D0094186

COUNTRY ROADS & SCENIC DRIVES IN THE MIDDLE ATLANTIC STATES

CHRISTINE M. BENTON

Produced by Book Developers, Inc.
of Chicago, Illinois,
for Contemporary Books, Inc.

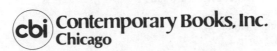 Contemporary Books, Inc.
Chicago

Library of Congress Cataloging in Publication Data

Benton, Chris.
    Country roads and scenic drives in the Middle Atlantic States.

    1. Middle Atlantic States—Description and travel—
Guide-books.   2. Automobiles—Road guides—Middle
Atlantic States.   I. Title.
F106.B44   917.4   78-57453
ISBN 0-8092-7514-7
ISBN 0-8092-7513-9 pbk.

Published by Contemporary Books, Inc.
180 North Michigan Avenue, Chicago, Illinois 60601
Manufactured in the United States of America
Library of Congress Catalog Card Number: 78-57453
International Standard Book Number: 0-8092-7514-7 (cloth)
                                    0-8092-7513-9 (paper)

Published simultaneously in Canada by
Beaverbooks
953 Dillingham Road
Pickering, Ontario L1W 1Z7
Canada

To Mike

Contents

Introduction

To many of us, driving the Mid-Atlantic states means cruising the interstate highways in a visual blur, our thoughts on nothing but getting there as quickly and painlessly as possible. To others, it means running daily errands along congested local roads, battling rush-hour traffic jams and road designs that went out with the Duesenberg. Time is a common roadblock, so we continue to melt into lanes of monotonous interstate traffic, persuading ourselves that the boredom and congestion are justified by the savings in time. Well, this may be true of driving in California; it may even be true of the Midwest. But, here in the germ of the nation, ancient canal towpaths and farm roads crisscross and loop around expressways and highways that were made for modern driving. Biggest isn't always best, especially when the selection is so varied. A low-speed road actually may save time over a rush-hour expressway. There are so many roads of all kinds, origins, and ages, in fact, that you can find a less traveled route almost anywhere—if you're willing to look.

The country roads included in this book are meant to guide local residents to some backwoods sites they may have missed in their mundane auto runs. The roads also provide good local tours for anyone from another area who is planning an extended sightseeing vacation to the Mid-Atlantic region. Most of these tours include lesser known attractions and avoid the most popular tourist sights. For the tourist sights that are worth seeing anyway, the book offers advice on off-season trips.

Looking is the secret to enjoyable driving in the Mid-Atlantic region. The very fact that the area is densely populated and highly developed in many spots gives emphasis to the delightful hidden nooks and crannies that you'll find all throughout the Mid-Atlantic—in Delaware, Maryland, New Jersey, New York, and Pennsylvania, and in Washington, D.C. One of the nicest features about the states and D.C. is that many 100- to 300-year-old structures are still standing, some of them next to contemporary buildings. Where the original structures themselves have failed to survive, historical societies and other concerned agencies have made the necessary moves to restore or even reconstruct these mirrors of our heritage.

Reconstruction efforts are being made in Mother Nature's domain as well as in the manmade America of the past. For example, strip-mined land in Pennsylvania is being reclaimed, the Hudson River is being cleaned up, and national natural landmarks are being designated every year, ensuring the future survival of this beautiful and fruitful area.

All this adds up to some great scenic driving—whether you're taking a long-distance trip, are out for a Sunday drive, or are just looking for a more picturesque route to your local grocery store. While you can make good time on some of the routes mentioned in the following chapters, the emphasis is definitely not on speed. I hope that the numerous detours, side trips, and roadside attractions will lure you out of your car. If nothing else, some of the purely scenic drives should relax you enough to induce you to cut your speed and soak up a little more of the view.

The Mid-Atlantic is a land of many faces, and to see them all, you'd have to spend years driving the area. Although many of the surface features are similar from state to state, each state actually offers a little something different, if you look carefully. This is not a land of wide-open spaces—it's a land largely dependent upon water and brimming with colonial history.

The waters include the Atlantic and its many sounds and bays; rivers, creeks, and springs; deep lakes and ponds. Surrounding them are lighthouses, boardwalks and piers, skipjacks and ocean liners, and fishing villages and lakeside resorts. To the north, the Mid-Atlantic is mountain country—deep-green forestlands full of miraculously preserved covered bridges, colonial taverns, and long-abandoned forts and the crumbling iron furnaces of a bygone industrial age. And forming the solid foundation of all of this is still a surprising amount of fruitful farmland. Among the rolling hills are the cheerful red farm buildings of Pennsylvania, the diverse old mills that sit alongside nearly every creek, and the patchwork velvet of neatly planted crops.

Besides the well-known cities of the Mid-Atlantic, you'll find every size and shape of human community you can imagine—modern suburbs, quaint fishing villages, crafts villages, religious settlements, one-horse farm towns, and even ghost towns.

An important thing to know is that driving in the Mid-Atlantic is different from driving elsewhere in the nation. If you're from the Midwest, the curves, peaks, dips, blind turns, and narrow lanes of the old roads may disconcert you. And if you're from the West, you may find yourself becoming impatient with the antiquated pavement and design. On many roads you'll really have to curb your speed and, in the winter, arm yourself with snow tires and your best judgment when driving the hillier areas.

Before you begin your drives, decide that you won't plan to do too much at once. Even when the scenery isn't optimum, the drive should be relaxing. Keep in mind that the drives outlined here—especially the extended ones—can take quite a long time to complete if you stop at every inviting attraction, so either select a series of stops ahead of time, or break a long tour into several daytrips, if your stay in one region is limited. If you find a route and area you like in particular, don't hesitate to blaze your own trail. You're almost guaranteed to find another country road not listed here. Treat the drives in the following chapters as starting points for an inside view of the best of the region.

To make it easier to choose a trip, each Mid-Atlantic state has been divided into sections based mainly on geography but also on the sometimes intangible flavor each area exudes. Atmosphere, terrain, and attractions are likely to overlap geographic boundaries, of course, but the divisions will give you a general idea of what is in store for you—and for your car.

What you're really about to experience and what should bring skeptics to the Mid-Atlantic is the unexpected. Residents will find backyard treasures, and out-of-towners will find myths dispelled when they are confronted with natural beauty in and around the cities. Again, each state has something individual to offer. New Jersey has the pristine Pine Barrens, a huge wilderness right in the middle of the Boston-to-Richmond megalopolis, whose very existence sometimes comes as a surprise to Easterners. In Maryland, you'll find a little of everything, from historic colonial to urban sprawl. This multifaceted state is the epitome of the Mid-Atlantic, with the American character, developed over a 300-year period, stamped on every acre. There are hidden corners, often overlooked by locals, never more than a mile or two away in Maryland. To those who have crossed the state many times on Route 70 or on the newer Route 40-48, the mountain gaps, colonial taverns, octagonal tollgate houses, and winding paths along old scenic Route 40, the National Pike, should make a delightful change.

In New York, the news is wilderness. There's a lot more to the state than New York City; even for city dwellers, country drives (away from the crowded resorts) are unexpectedly close to Gotham. The surprise in Pennsylvania is the forest-shrouded remains of an earlier farm era—stoical covered bridges painted a cheerful barn red, the stone ruins of old iron furnaces and, perhaps most fascinating of all, ghost towns that reflect the easy-come, easy-go industrial booms of yesteryear—deserted coal towns, abandoned iron communities, and old Indian campsites. You may even discover your own favorite relic or ruins. Finally, in the Mid-Atlantic's "little finger," Delaware, the atmosphere is similar to most of the Mid-Atlantic, but the manmade attractions are fewer and farther between, and natural sights are less spectacular. The surprise here is the peace and quiet. Delaware's resorts attract an older set and offer unbelievable tranquility, while the farms and rural communities take a low-key approach to tourism. Delaware is country roads personified and really should be explored according to your own whims.

Every region of every Mid-Atlantic state really does have

something to offer, and although not every county is represented here, I have attempted to give a good sample of the basic "neighborhoods" in each state. Counties not represented are just as worthy of exploration by car, but the route planning is up to you. Volumes could be written about the area without covering everything of note.

To follow the directions given in the following chapters it's helpful, although not really necessary, to use local road maps. Route numbers can be confusing, so a map does help. Unless otherwise noted, all route numbers are state or county roads; U.S. and interstate highways are designated as such. Pay special attention to Pennsylvania's route system—the abbreviation "Leg. Route" means "legislative route" and refers to secondary highways with five-digit numbers. Where possible, I have included the word-names of numbered routes, although they may change from town to town on one route. In asking for local directions, be sure to state clearly by number which route you are seeking. Many roads in the Mid-Atlantic are known to locals by several different names—a route number, a street name, and sometimes an old name that was given to them during their seventeenth-, eighteenth-, and nineteenth-century use. You'll also find many roads that are former Indian trails. Even a six-lane highway may follow the same basic route as a trail followed by the first Americans 400 years ago. While this may be confusing to the out-of-towner trying to work through a maze of routes, it only adds to the potential for soaking up history. As you travel these roads, keep in mind that they may have been traveled by generations of early Americans, and enrich your trip by learning the story of this colonial frontier before you set out. You'll see some things here that you can't see anywhere else—but only if you're willing to look.

1

Delaware

There's only one state in the Union smaller in area than Delaware (it's Rhode Island), and although several have smaller populations, few states seem to be forgotten as often. Delaware is probably the least recognized today of all the 13 original colonies. This is not because it is any less scenic than the other Mid-Atlantic states, nor is it less important, because today it puts food on our tables and gives us a place to go for a peaceful vacation. But still we hear little of Delaware. It sounds like *ideal* territory for country roads. And that's exactly what they are in this state—quiet or even invisible routes through a state that scorns ostentation.

Perhaps Delaware should be nicknamed the Quiet State. Any drive through its nonurban areas is bound to be relatively traffic-free, offering a relaxing trip. You'll find fewer roadside historic sites, and you may have to drive for a longer stretch to take in more than one point of interest. What Delaware does offer is peace and quiet. A large portion of the state's 2,057 square miles are put to the plow, and if you're driving the length of the state on a highway, tilled fields or growing crops are mostly what you'll see. The terrain is flat, much of it resembling the type of land you'll find in New Jersey's farm country.

A typical secondary highway in the central section is lined with farms on one side and alluring forests of pine and holly on the other. You'll come upon an occasional house and yard carved out of the roadside forest and some tempting dirt or sand roads disappearing into the trees. Unfortunately, many of these roads are private driveways, posted with "No Trespassing" signs. The signs, of course, should be heeded, and you should drive on with optimism and a sharp eye out for public paths.

For other scenic drives, try the shore routes. For stops along the way, try exiting at any of the towns along the north-south highways. Produce stands offering the local bounty—tomatoes, corn, squashes, greens—are all over, and you'll find antique shops in the least likely places. Again, put your best tire forward to get the most out of Delaware.

It won't take long to drive through Delaware if you're crossing state lines, so you won't have to stay overnight. If you choose to, though, make hotel arrangements in advance. Towns can be spaced far apart, and many of them are quite small. In the winter, many hotels, restaurants, and other tourist attractions are closed. Some good restaurants are available, but they, too, can be few and far between. Seafood is the feature, and it's probably the shore resorts that have the best eateries. If you're driving north and you want to stop for a delicious meal before you enter Delaware, stop at the Crab Shack. Just south of the Delaware Memorial Bridge, this unassuming restaurant has genuinely fresh seafood and some of the best fried oysters I've ever tasted. It makes a great luncheon stop and isn't likely to be crowded.

The most scenically interesting region of the state is undoubtedly the coast, the southeastern corner in particular. Like the shores of Maryland and New Jersey, the beaches are a mixture of resorts and wildlife refuges and can be crowded during swimming season.

Scenic drives

Route 9: about 60 miles through New Castle and Kent Counties. From Delaware Memorial Bridge to Kitts Hummock driving the quiet seashore.

If you have always imagined that there really is nothing to Delaware but farms, try driving State Route 9 along the coastline. The trip can be done in a couple of hours, taking leisurely driving into account. Start on Route 9 from the Delaware Memorial Bridge and go south along the Delaware River and Bay. The most interesting section of the trip is near Bombay Hook National Wildlife Refuge, about 35 miles along the way.

Past the wildlife refuge and about five miles west of Route 9 is Dover, the state capital. The State House was built in 1787, and there are several other historic sites to take in while you're there, including Old Christ Church.

Just past Dover Air Force Base, Route 9 joins U.S. Route 113, and you can end your trip here. Or drive east on the main road to the small village of Kitts Hummock on the shore.

Ocean Drive revisited: about 30 miles through Sussex County. From Lewes to the Maryland line—continuing New Jersey's Ocean Drive through Delaware and Maryland.

For seashore freaks, the New Jersey Ocean Drive from Atlantic City to Cape May Point can be extended through Delaware and Maryland. For that matter, it can be extended as far south as you care to go, but for Mid-Atlantic drivers, the trip ends around Ocean City, Maryland. (See *Southeast New Jersey* for details on Ocean Drive.)

Start on Route 1, which is about three miles west of Lewes from the ferry. For a Lewes stopover, you can use Cape Henlopen's campsite. Drive about six miles south on Route 1 to reach the seashore, passing Henlopen Acres to Rehoboth Beach and Dewey Beach. These are resort towns and just as popular as those of Maryland and New Jersey. From here, drive about 11 miles—surrounded on both sides by water—to Bethany Beach, another resort town. Although the Delaware seashore is similar in many ways to that of Maryland and New Jersey, like the rest of the state, it offers understated versions of New Jersey's Atlantic City and Maryland's Ocean City. The three "beach towns"—Rehoboth, Dewey, and Bethany—form a short string of small resorts. There's the usual mixture of seafood restaurants and night clubs, old summer homes and high-rise condominiums, but the entire feeling is toned down. Vacationers come here to relax, many of them called back to this peaceful hideaway year after year.

From Bethany Beach it's about six miles to the Maryland line. The first town you'll reach is Maryland Beach, where Route 1 becomes Route 528. Seven or eight miles south of Maryland Beach is Ocean City, the Atlantic City of Maryland. Its detractors call it somewhat seedy, but, as at Atlantic City, its admirers flock to the beach faithfully every year.

For an extension of the extension, try a side trip to Assateague Island (see *Southeast Maryland* for details).

Country roads

Because of the nature of the state, country roads can be found everywhere in Delaware. Exit off any main road or highway and you'll find antique shops, farm stands, and junk shops. Local crafts are sometimes sold from private homes. A self-guided jaunt is likely to yield a hand-carved duck decoy, a decorative doo-dad made of local pine cones, a jar of inimitable beach plum jelly, a box of saltwater taffy, or a great piece of "refinishable" furniture.

Wherever you decide to wander, remember that in Delaware, the off-season is really off. Most of the establishments that thrive during the summer—restaurants, antique shops and the like—close their doors in October and stay closed until May.

I really believe the best country roads in Delaware are those you discover yourself. But, for the record, the following paths are good starting points. From these routes, head for the "back-back roads," some of which can be explored only in an "oversand" vehicle. If you don't own your own jeep, check out rentals in the beach towns. Almost any area near the beaches in the south is worth exploring; other individual attractions in the state include historic sites and some interesting wildlife refuges.

Country jaunts—Sussex County

The beach area's many antique shops and other emporia can be found by driving in any one of several directions. For example, try taking Route 54 west along the state's southern border, from the tiny town of Fenwick Island as far as Maryland's Wicomico County, near the Nanticoke River. Or start at Seaport Antiques in Fenwick Island. During the summer the owner holds Sunday fleamarkets in the barn.

Other good antique jaunts can be made by taking Route 3 or Route 5 north to south, about 25 miles to Millsboro. Route 30 begins south of Milford near Lincoln, and Route 5 starts off Route 1, north of Milton. At the intersection of U.S. Route 9, the two join, proceeding south to Millsboro.

You can choose from many bayside trips by starting at Millsboro and driving along either the north or south bank of the intricate Indian River Bay. Small local parks available for picnicking line the shores, and the routes can be quite scenic.

In the western portion of the county, try following Route 577 southeast from Federalsburg, Maryland, to Delaware's Woodland. It's only about an eight-mile drive, and Woodland has an interesting little ferry that crosses the Nanticoke River.

Other short—and sometimes rugged—back roads may be found off the ocean drive, Route 1 (or 14) from Rehoboth Beach to Bethany Beach. You'll see the now-deserted stone towers from which World War II Americans watched for submarines. Along Indian River Bay, where there is an ocean outlet, you'll find anglers fishing for the ugly sand sharks. There are parking areas off the road and some intriguing sand roads into the dunes; oversand vehicles are necessary on many of them.

New Castle and Kent counties

A short scenic drive in northern Delaware runs from Maryland's Chesapeake City to Delaware City. From Chesapeake City, follow Route 285 and other local roads east along the north bank of the old Chesapeake and Delaware Canal, which connects those two bays over about 15 miles of land. The Canal National Wildlife Refuge lines the banks, and campsites are available.

For a city retreat of sorts, try King Street, in downtown Wilmington. The old street market in the middle of DuPont country is worth seeing. About six miles south of the city on Route 52 is Winterthur, the 200-room DuPont estate. Furnished in styles popular from the 1640s to the 1840s, the house is open to complete tours by reservation only. But even without a reservation, you can stop in and look over ten of the rooms.

An interesting site in the Dover area is Dover Downs, in the town of Harrington, where you can see harness racing. About 18 miles south of Dover, at the intersection of U.S. Routes 13 and 14, is a good point from which to take Route 14 east, running into Route 1 and the Ocean Drive.

2

Maryland

Cross-state drives

Independence Trail: 120 miles through Baltimore, Anne Arundel, and Calvert counties. Mason-Dixon Line to Calvert Cliffs—following history's path through central Maryland.

This north-to-south route through the center of Maryland gives auto travelers a real taste of colonial America. From the Pennsylvania border all the way south to Cove Point in Calvert County, you will pass unaltered and beautifully restored structures that tell the story of Maryland's childhood. Tucked into the Chesapeake Bay area and the metropolitan sprawls of Baltimore and Washington, D.C., are the vestiges of those rough years—tiny churches, time-worn travelers' inns, stoical lighthouses, stately mansions, and the former homes of heroes of the Revolutionary and Civil wars.

Some of the roads on this tour are heavily traveled and not as scenic as you might desire. Nevertheless, these developed areas often offer sightseeing opportunities that will lure you out of your car. It's best to take this trip during the summer, perhaps as a vacation-on-wheels, with overnight stops along the way. If you prefer, you can break the tour into several short trips, but if you have decided to stop overnight anywhere, be sure to plan ahead and make hotel reservations before you set out.

Although the emphasis is on history along these roads, there are scattered natural attractions as well, along with some truly breathtaking panoramic views. The north-to-south route gives you a look at most of the types of land you'll find in Maryland with the exception of the mountains in the west. North of Baltimore you'll find rolling hills, waterfalls, and streams. Around Annapolis, the land is relatively flat, and the main attractions are the bay and the tidewater rivers that cut into the coast. Farther south, you will pass through Maryland's fertile tobacco country and on to the quaint fishing villages of southern Maryland.

The most interesting sights on this trip probably are the scores of churches that fill the state. Many of Maryland's early settlers were drawn to the state for its religious tolerance, and today you'll find churches of all denominations, some founded 250 years ago. The churches range in size and stature from cathedrals to the little chapels of ease erected for the settlers who lived far from the colonial cities of Maryland.

Begin your trip on Route 45 at the Pennsylvania border. Route 45 runs parallel to U.S. Route 83 and makes a good alternate route for that highway. The town of Maryland Line is a good place to get onto Route 45, and from there south to Baltimore the road runs through the Gunpowder Falls and Gunpowder State Park area, along the river of that name. Drive about 15 miles to the Glencoe-Sparks-Phoenix area. Near Sparks, you'll pass Milton Inn, a tavern built of native stone in 1740. Route 45 used to be York Road, a major route for colonial travelers, and Milton Inn served as a rest stop for those settlers. At one time, the inn was converted into a Friends School, and John Wilkes Booth was one of its students. Once again serving as an inn, the building has charming interiors, with stone walls and huge fireplaces. *Life* magazine once distinguished the Milton Inn as one of America's most interesting eating places.

At this point you can cross Route 83 on Route 129 west to

visit the National Association of Handcraftsmen, Inc. You'll find the association in the Hunt Valley Inn on Shawan Road, where exhibits of native crafts are changed every two months.

Back on Route 45, drive south another five miles to Lutherville. At 1301 York Road, you can visit the Fire Museum, which boasts more than 40 pieces of hand-drawn, horse-drawn, and motorized fire-fighting gear, some pieces dating back to the early 1800s. The museum is open to the public on Saturday and Sunday afternoons.

From Lutherville, drive a few miles to Towson, where you'll find several historic sites. The stone milkhouse on Old York Road (Route 45), is an interesting structure which now houses an antique shop. The mother and daughter who own the shop wear Victorian dress, giving you the feeling you're in a museum, rather than just a shop.

Off York Road you will find the Hampton House on Hampton Lane. This national historic site was built between 1783 and 1790 in the late Georgian style. If you'd like to see the original Empire and Federal furnishings of the mansion, you can take a guided tour of the interior during the afternoon, Tuesday through Sunday.

From Towson, follow the Baltimore Beltway (Route 695) east. While much of Baltimore is less than gorgeous, the city does offer some worthwhile tourist sights (see Chapter 7 for details on Baltimore City). From this point, take route 151 and Route 20 to Edgemere on the bay. There you can investigate Fort Howard. Or continue on Route 695 and exit at Route 3 south. This is not the most scenic part of the tour, but it does take you through Severn Run State Park, where you can stop for a picnic.

From Route 3, take Route 178 east at Door's Cor. Keep an eye out for Crownsville State Hospital. Incongruously placed next door is St. Paul's Chapel, built in 1865. It's easy to miss this small board-and-batten frame building that sits in the shadow of the huge hospital. The architecture is simple, with a plain belfry on top.

Continue on Route 178 to Route 50-301. You can either drive northeast on Route 50-301 to Annapolis (see *Country roads* under *Southern Maryland,* page) or southwest to Route 2. Route 2 takes you across the pretty South River to Edgewater. Note the change in atmosphere as you cross the bridge—it almost seems like a gateway to the real South. The woods here are thick and the trees weighted with vines; the communities combine a suburban and rural flavor. The South River is a popular place, drawing duck hunters and other vacationers from the D. C. metropolitan area. For the through-driver, there are several points of interest.

To reach the London Town Publik House and Gardens, take Route 253 to London Town Road in Edgewater. The "publik house," built around 1745, is a two-story brick inn—the last remnant of a once-prosperous town. In its heyday the inn was on the route from Philadelphia to Williamsburg and was reached by crossing the South River on a ferry. Thomas Jefferson crossed that ferry in 1775. Today visitors can see this national historic landmark daily between 10:00 A.M. and 4:00 P.M. The natural woodland gardens overlooking the river are worth visiting.

As you pass the town of South River, look for the South River Club off Route 2. Although it is not open to the public, you can see it from the road. Records call this the first club established by the English settlers and the oldest continually used social club in the United States. The original clubhouse was destroyed by fire in 1740, but the club has been rebuilt in its original style.

Continue south on Route 2 to Davidsonville. At the intersection of Route 2 and Brick Church Road, you'll find All Hallows Church, which is open on request. The 1710 church has its original exterior and a restored interior. Check the bell in the rustic tower, dated 1727.

Farther south on Route 2, at Tracy's Landing, is another old church. Near the intersection of Route 258, St. James Church was built in 1763, but it's the graveyard that deserves the most attention. The grave of Christopher Birkhead's wife, dated 1665, is the oldest known grave in the state.

Just north of the Calvert County line, you can detour off Route 2 to Route 261, continuing your drive along the Chesapeake Bay past the towns of Rose Haven, North Beach, and Chesapeake Beach. Or you can stay on Route 2 to Sunderland. At the intersection of Routes 2 and 4, you'll find All Saints Church. Built in 1774, the Episcopal church is made of Flemish bond brick walls and a sandstone front that was imported from England in 1735.

If you detoured off Route 2 to get onto Route 261, you can now take Route 263 back to Route 2. If you stayed on Route 2 to get to Sunderland, continue along Route 2-4 to Prince Frederick, a good departure point for several side trips.

South of Prince Frederick, take Route 2 to Route 506 (Sixes Road), where you'll drive through Battle Creek Cypress Swamp, which has been named a natural landmark because of the unusual location of these typically southern trees. These glorious trees are from 50 to 100 feet tall, and their intriguing bark ranges in color from silver to cinnamon red.

Return to Route 2-4, and take Route 264 south to Broome's Island. On Broome's Island Road, you'll find Christ Church, built in 1772. If you have time to stop, check out the unique garden, said to be planted according to a Bible story. Also in Broome's Island is a small oyster fleet that you can see, along with Denton Oyster Packing Plant, which is open (on advance notice) between October and March.

South of Broome's Island, Route 2-4 takes you to the beautiful Calvert Cliffs area, which combines outdoor recreation, delightful panoramas, and historic sites. In Lusby you can visit the Calvert Cliffs Nuclear Power Museum. This barn holds exhibits on the natural history and agriculture of the area. There is a viewing platform here that lets you look out over the broad expanse of Chesapeake Bay. You can also see the ruins of Preston's Cliff, former home of Richard Preston, also known as the "great Quaker." Of special note is the north end of the house, which was built between 1687 and 1691.

For hikers, Calvert Cliffs State Park has a two-and-a-half mile, one-way trail. These spectacular cliffs, discovered by Captain John Smith in 1608, run 30 miles along the bay and reach heights of 40 to 120 feet. Scientists have found tons of Miocene epoch fossils 12 to 15 million years old imbedded in the

(Above) Wild Calvert Cliffs are a popular site in southern Maryland. (Below) Calvert Cliffs' Cove Point Lighthouse is the oldest tower light on Chesapeake Bay.

cliffs, but fossil digging by visitors is not allowed.

Finally, in Lusby, you'll come upon Middleham Chapel. This 1748 Episcopal church, the oldest cruciform structure in the state, has a chapel bell dated 1699.

From the cliffs, take Route 2-4 to Route 497 east. At the end of Cove Point Road you will spot Cove Point Lighthouse. Run by the Coast Guard, Cove Point is the oldest tower light on the bay. Visitors may go inside on any day except Monday.

Return to Route 2-4 and drive south to Solomons. If you have the time, spend an afternoon here. You can visit the 1870 Solomons United Methodist Church, which has a pulpit with hand-carved arches made from the timbers of an old sailing schooner's captain's cabin. There is also St. Peter's, an Episcopal chapel built for the area fishermen and others who work on the water, and the only board-and-batten type of church in Calvert County.

Your last stop should be at Calvert Maritime Museum, where you can spend time exploring the museum's displays on four waterfront acres. There you will find the Old Solomons Schoolhouse, with exhibits on local maritime history, fossil samples taken from Calvert Cliffs, log canoes, and a historic lighthouse— Drum Point Light. Built in 1883, the lighthouse is one of three surviving screw-pile lights on Chesapeake Bay. You can visit it any day but Monday.

WESTERN MARYLAND (Vacationland of Presidents)

Scenic drives

Route 219: about 40 miles through Garrett County. From Keyser's Ridge to Redhouse—driving Maryland's mountain country, the vacationland of presidents.

If you prefer mountain views and crystal-blue lakes to the sandy beach and salt air of the other Maryland, this is the tour for you. Garrett County is famous for its resorts, which served as summer vacation homes for several U.S. presidents.

Garrett is a corner county, offering interstate routes and a little flavor of both Pennsylvania and West Virginia.

Start your tour at Keyser's Ridge, easily accessible from Route 48, Route 40, or Route 219, all of which meet just a few miles south of the Pennsylvania border. Take Route 219 south and prepare yourself for some breathtaking views. The road travels over the Allegheny Mountain plateau, giving drivers a panorama of the picturesque farmland from the highway's 2,800-foot height. This area, called The Cove, features a scenic overlook a couple of miles north of the town of Accident.

Also north of Accident is a town called Friendsville. The sign to that town will take you off Route 219. If it's summertime, you may be able to hear the Friendsville Old Time Fiddlers' Contest, held on the third Saturday in July. In the area also is Bear Creek Rearing Station, which offers a look at fish in all stages of development. To reach it, turn right off Route 219 at the Friendsville sign and right again at Accident-Bear Creek Road.

South of Accident, you will drive by George Hill—elevation 2,946 feet. The next town you will pass is McHenry, with Wisp Ski Area to your right (west). The road then crosses Deep Creek Lake, the site of a state park that attracts all types of outdoorsmen. Maryland's biggest lake, it has 65 miles of shoreline, where visitors may boat, swim, waterski, fish, hike, and ride horseback in summer. In winter there is a full range of cold-weather sports. You'll find the entrance to the park four miles south of the lake's northern edge, at Cherry Creek Road. Some great nature walks begin at the park.

From there, it's six-and-a-half miles to Swallow Falls State Forest. Stop here and revel in the glories of Swallow Falls and Muddy Creek Falls. The latter is an awesome cascade of water pouring over 51 feet of rocks.

In another six miles you'll reach Oakland, Garrett's county seat. This is the vacationland of presidents, tucked in between Deep Creek Lake and Backbone Mountain. For sightseers, there are some interesting historic sites, such as the B & O Railroad Station on Green Street. Although the existing station was built in 1884, the depot has been receiving and sending off trains since

Muddy Creek Falls is one of the main attractions at Garrett County's Swallow Falls State Park.

1851. On Second Street you can see the Church of the Presidents, so named for the attendance of Presidents Grant, Harrison, and Cleveland during their vacation stays in Oakland. Also of interest is the Garrett County Historical Museum on Center Street. If you plan an extended stay in Oakland, you might be interested in stopping off at Western Trails, Inc. This organization offers horseback riding and hayrides through the area and can direct you to camping facilities.

Drive another six miles south and you'll reach the town of Redhouse, near the West Virginia border.

The formative years: about 45 miles through Carroll County. From Westminster to Terra Rubra—view farms and homesteads, mills and mansions of a land almost untouched by modern development.

If you are not interested in the scenery, you should at least drive through northern Carroll County to see the results of a spectacular restoration/preservation effort. This short tour winds through pretty farm country that combines structures of every age—from the farm buildings of the late eighteenth century to the homes of today. Besides well-preserved buildings, there also are the legacies left by some well-known figures from the American past—Francis Scott Key, General Meade of the Civil War, John Carroll, and others.

Start your Carroll County tour at the Carroll County Farm Museum south of Westminster. The museum can be reached by turning left from Route 104 onto Center Street, about a mile south of Westminster. This living museum is closed between October and April, but if you're there during the summer, you will have the chance to watch some colonial activities: spinning, broom-making, tinsmithing, and the making of apple butter, for example. It all takes place in the cheery red-wood-and-brick

The Carroll County Farm Museum is one of many working, living museums in the Mid-Atlantic region.

farm buildings. On 140 acres are a farmhouse built in 1852, a smokehouse, a springhouse and other outbuildings, in addition to such accoutrements of the era as horse-drawn buggies.

Drive north to Westminster, where you can visit Carroll County Jail on Court Street, built in 1837. You can also see the county courthouse, built in 1838. To round out your Westminster visit, head for the historical society building, circa 1807, at 206 East Main Street.

Leave Westminster via Route 27 and drive 10 miles to Route 30, about a mile north of Manchester. Turn left on Route 30 to find a good example of the brick-end barns that were once scattered across the county. The design of these unique barns was borrowed from the Pennsylvania Dutch.

Follow Route 30 a few more miles farther to Deep Run Road and turn left. Five miles takes you back to Route 140 and to Union Mills. For history buffs, the Union Mills Homestead, also known as the Shriver Homestead Museum, is a must-see. Built in 1797, this 23-room, Z-shaped homestead is a miracle of preservation. The Shriver family lived in the house until 1970, making a tremendous effort to hold onto *everything* that belonged to the original household. The result is a truly authentic homestead of that era, including the original grist and sawmill the Shrivers built on Pipe Creek. Visitors can explore the homestead between May and November.

From Union Mills, take route 140 south about six miles to Westminster and turn right onto Route 97, about one-half mile from the town. Turn left onto Uniontown Road and drive about five miles to Uniontown.

Uniontown is another amazing piece of restoration work. It is distinguished as the only whole town in the state to be named a registered national historic district. The reason for the distinction is that the town has changed hardly at all over the last hundred years. The peaceful, tree-shaded streets are lined with colonial-type houses, many of them the typical white wood with black shutters. For a closer look at them, park your car and walk.

Leaving Uniontown, turn right on Route 84. Three miles south of Taneytown, take a look at Trevanion, an 1817 mansion

The rambling Shriver Homestead Museum is a major attraction in Carroll County's Union Mills.

constructed in a combination of Victorian and Italian styles. This truly massive structure originally had 35 rooms, 88 windows, and 16 chimneys.

About three miles north is Taneytown, where you will find another estate on the left-hand side of Trevanion Road. Antrim is an 1844 mansion, notable for its cupola, which was used as a lookout by General Meade while he was headquartered there prior to the Battle of Gettysburg.

From Taneytown turn left (southwest) on Crouse Mill Road and drive five miles to Uniontown Road. Turn right on Uniontown Road, drive one mile, and turn right on Route 194. In half a mile you'll reach Keysville-Bruceville Road, where you turn left. On the right side of the street, about one and one-third miles down, you'll find Terra Rubra, the birthplace of Francis Scott Key. The original house was destroyed by a storm in 1770 and rebuilt in 1850. The monument to Key, who composed the "Star-Spangled Banner," was erected on the grounds in 1915.

Country roads

Route 15: about 25 miles through Frederick County.

This north-south tour from the Pennsylvania border to the city of Frederick incorporates scenes typical of this part of western Maryland—covered bridges, iron furnaces, mountain views, creeks and, again, well-preserved historic sites.

Start the tour in Emmitsburg, about a mile south of the Mason-Dixon line. The first place to stop is Mount St. Mary's College, established in 1808. There you can visit the Grotto of Lourdes replica on the mountain peak. The first national Catholic shrine in the country, the grotto contains a calming garden path that leads to the Stations of the Cross.

Drive a couple of miles south on Route 15 to find a scenic overlook where you can park your car. About four miles south of the overlook (one mile north of Thurmont), turn right on Roddy Road. Roddy Road will lead you to a King Post truss-supported covered bridge, built over Owens Creek between 1850 and 1860.

Emmitsburg's Grotto of Lourdes replica provides a moment of peaceful retreat.

From Thurmont, you can travel west on Route 77, which leads to Catoctin Mountain National Park and Cunningham Falls State Park (see the *Old Hagerstown-Westminster Turnpike,* page 000). Or drive six miles south of Thurmont to Catoctin at the intersection of Route 806. About half a mile north of the intersection is Catoctin Furnace, a historic district. This iron furnace, built in 1774 and used until 1905, is now being restored.

For the kiddies, you can turn off on Route 806 to Catoctin Mountain Zoo. The privately owned petting zoo, situated in a natural woodland setting, boasts one of the largest American collections of lemurs.

Drive a few miles south to Old Frederick Road, south of Lewistown, and turn right. Here you'll find another covered bridge. Built over Fishing Creek between 1850 and 1860, this one is a Bowstring and Howe truss-supported bridge.

A Frederick County covered bridge.

Another six miles takes you to Frederick, which is known as one of the most history-packed cities in the state. Like Uniontown in Carroll County, Frederick has a whole section that looks as it did 150 to 200 years ago. From there, you can ask anybody in town where the historic sites are. Frederick has many of them, providing a good day's walk through history.

Old Hagerstown-Westminster Turnpike (Route 77): about 20 miles through Frederick County.

Route 77, once known as the Hagerstown-Westminster Turnpike, divides scenic Catoctin Mountain National Park and Cunningham State Park, both on the Catoctin Ridge. In the days before the auto, this road was a major connecting route with the National Pike, Route 40. Today it is a minor highway running through beautiful country and a perfect spot for a leisurely drive or a visit to one of the parks.

Start in Thurmont at the intersection of Routes 77 and 15. Take Route 77 west to Catoctin Mountain Park. You'll find a visitor center at Park Central Road, where you can pick up information and directions. The park offers a seven-mile, marked auto tour that you can follow, or you can blaze your own trail on the park roads. Following is a general tour of the parks, which you can alter according to your time and desires.

Turn right on Park Central Road and drive by Blue Blazes and Whiskey Still to Misty Mountain. The road then curves sharply to the left. Around the curve are several parking lots that serve as overlooks from the 1,500-foot height. Once past the bend, you'll see Camp David, where the elevation is 1,880 feet, and Greentop. The labeled tour starts at Manahan Road, if you should decide to follow it.

From Catoctin Mountain Park, return to Route 77 and drive east to Catoctin Hollow Road. Turn right and stop at the 1,000-foot scenic overlook near Hunting Creek Lake. Drive by Mink Farm Road. From here on, the road runs parallel with Hunting Creek, intersecting Route 15 near Catoctin Furnace.

Parks and battlefields: about 30 miles through Washington County.

Washington County is chock-full of national battlefields, parks, monuments, and memorials to Civil War heroes. Besides the fact that it is in the National Pike territory, the land between Frederick, Hagerstown, and Harpers Ferry has seen a lot of action. Civil War buffs could spend weeks here, just soaking up all the history.

This tour takes you in a small circle through the battlefield territory, principally on secondary highways and back roads. There are a lot of sights to see and a lot of recreation opportunities, so plan your trip according to the attractions that appeal to you.

Start at Greenbrier State Park, which you can reach from U.S. Route 40 east, about 10 miles east of Hagerstown. The park is 1,200 acres of blue-mountain land, with a scenic mountain gap in its northeast corner. There's a lake as well as a forest rich in wildlife to explore. Visitors can picnic, boat, swim, fish, or hike at the park.

Leave Greenbrier, via Route 20, and get onto Route 66 south. Take Route 66 south to Alternate Route 40 and the town of Boonsboro. Turn right on Route 34, also known as the Boonsboro Pike, and drive one mile west to Crystal Grottoes Caverns.

Continuing west on Route 34, you'll reach Antietam National Battlefield Site. The battlefield covers 810 acres (12 square miles) and you can see the whole thing by driving along the eight miles of roads through the park. The site is laid out and marked to allow visitors to travel the path that the battling armies followed during six fateful hours on September 17, 1862. In three grueling phases the Federal Army fought to force Lee's army back into Virginia. Lee did retreat, and the tide turned in the Civil War.

This stark view of Antietam Battlefield in Washington County zeroes in on ghostly Bloody Lane.

But the cost was great: 15 percent of the Federal soldiers and 26 percent of the Confederate soldiers were killed or wounded in the struggle.

You can follow the chronological sequence of the battle phases by touring the site from north to south. One of the most interesting spots on the battlefield is Burnside Bridge. To reach it, turn left off Route 34 on Rodman Avenue and left again toward the Sherrick Farm, when Rodman turns into Branch Avenue. Built over Antietam Creek in 1836, the bridge was a key battle site in 1862 and today is a good example of the stone bridges found in Washington County.

From Antietam, take Route 34 west to about a mile west of Sharpsburg. There you can explore the C & O Canal and an old

The War Correspondents' Memorial is the focal point of Gathland State Park, just a few miles north of West Virginia's famous Harpers Ferry.

plantation called Ferry Hill Place. An alternate jaunt takes you to the Antietam Iron Works. To find it, return to Sherrick Farm from Burnside Bridge and turn left on Branch Avenue to Harpers Ferry Road. Turn left on Harpers Ferry Road and drive about two miles west of Sharpsburg.

About eight miles south of Antietam, you'll find the C & O Canal Lock 33, and the Salty Dog Tavern. The site is directly across the Potomac from historic Harpers Ferry in West Virginia, and the Salty Dog Tavern is the attraction here. Notorious since it opened its doors in the nineteenth century, the tavern also was a Prohibition era moonshine supply point.

From Harpers Ferry Road, drive east to Route 67 and proceed north to the town of Gapland. Turn right on Gapland Road to Gathland State Park. Located six miles south of Boonsboro and three-quarters of a mile east of Route 67, the unique park was a retreat built by a Civil War correspondent named Townsend in the late nineteenth century. Townsend became a well-known journalist and novelist after the war, and the park is named for his nom de plume—Gath. The most interesting structure still standing on the grounds is the large stone arch Townsend erected as a memorial to his fellow war correspondents.

CENTRAL MAR *f*LAND (Colonial Heritage)

Scenic drives

Capital circle tour: about 250 miles through Howard, Montgomery, and Prince George's counties. From Arabian horses to tobacco barns—a three-day weekend of Maryland heritage, with something for everyone.

This long, zigzagging circle tour of central Maryland really does offer something for everyone. Never straying far from the metropolitan area of Washington, D.C., the tour takes you over highways and country roads, where modern recreation facilities can be found near 200-year-old mansions and wildlife preserves are next door to the horse and tobacco farms that were started by Maryland's founding fathers.

In several places, the tour runs over major highways; you can avoid these, if you like, by taking parallel country roads of your choice. Sections of the long trip can be cut out altogether, or you can break the trip up into several afternoon jaunts. It does make an ideal sightseeing tour for visitors who are new to Maryland, showing some of just about everything there is to see in the state and providing attractions for each member of the family as well.

For a full sightseeing tour of the area, you might want to take a side trip to Washington, D.C., where you could easily spend a week exploring the nation's capital. To find the little-known corners of D.C., see Chapter 7.

Start this tour on Route 117 west, west of the town of Boyds. Drive straight on Barnesville Road to the Arabian Horse Museum (closed on Mondays). For a bird's-eye view of these beautiful creatures, turn left on Route 109 in Barnesville (about three miles from the museum). On the left, is Al-Marah Arabian Horse Farm, where 300 horses are raised on 2,000 acres of prime Maryland land. This is the largest Arabian horse farm in the country.

Continue on Route 109 to Beallsville, about three miles south. Turn left (east) on Route 28 and drive 15 or 20 miles to Rockville, the Montgomery County seat. Rockville became the county seat in 1776, and this pleasant town has three main historic districts that are best explored on foot—North Adams Street, West Montgomery Avenue, and South Washington Street.

On leaving Rockville, turn right on Route 189 south and drive seven miles to Great Falls on the Potomac River. This is a beautiful spot; if you stop here during the less popular seasons— late fall or early spring—you'll be rewarded by being able to make an almost solitary exploration of the rocks hanging over the rushing falls. Great Falls is a really peaceful spot, too; the roaring water drowns out most of the sounds of nearby civilization. While you're there you can stop in at the Chesapeake and Ohio Canal Museum, built in 1828 as an inn and lockhouse.

From the falls, turn right on MacArthur Boulevard to Glen Echo—about eight miles distant. Then turn left on Route 614,

The Potomac River's Great Falls is one of the prettiest sights in the Washington, D.C., area.

right on Route 396, and right on Oxford Road. On Oxford Road is the Clara Barton House, where the famous nurse lived and founded the American Red Cross. Nearby is Glen Echo Amusement Park, where you can picnic or divert the kids.

Turn right on MacArthur Boulevard and then right on Wilson Lane (Route 188). Take a left at River Road (Route 190) and follow the signs to the Washington Beltway—Route 495. You can skip this highway if you prefer back roads, especially if the weather is bad. Truckers call the beltway "Suicide Circle," mainly because it becomes extremely slippery when wet and tends to get icy in the winter. As an alternative to the beltway, take a side trip into the capital (see Chapter 7 for details on country roads), or drive along the Virginia banks of the Potomac. If you take the beltway, get off at Exit 37B and drive south to Route 210. Follow Route 210 to Oxon Hill Road and turn right to visit Oxon Hill Children's Farm.

Return to Route 210 south and take a right on Fort Washington Road. At the end of the road (seven miles from Oxon Hill) is Fort Washington National Park. Established on the east bank of the Potomac in 1797, this is one of the oldest American military installations. The existing fort was built in 1824.

Return to Route 210 and drive south to Accokeek. At the intersection of Routes 210 and 373, turn right on Bryan Point Road to the river. About 17 miles from Fort Washington is Colonial National Farm Museum. One of the many living museums in the Mid-Atlantic, this is a working example of an eighteenth-century freeholder's farm, open to visitors during the summer.

Return to Accokeek and take Route 373 across Route 210. Where Routes 223 and 373 fork, turn left on Route 223, about 13 miles to Clinton. In Clinton is the home of the infamous Mary Suratt. John Wilkes Booth is said to have stopped there after Lincoln's assassination, and Mary Suratt was hanged for conspiracy. The house is now being restored.

Continue on Route 223 to Route 408 and turn right. Drive about 10 miles to the fascinating town of Upper Marlboro. The town became Prince George's county seat in 1706 and has been a tobacco trade center for just about as long. At the county courthouse in town there is a plaque commemorating the birthplace of John Carroll, who was named the first Roman Catholic archbishop of the United States in 1808. If you drive through town between mid-April and the end of June, you can observe one of the time-honored tobacco auctions that have taken place here for years. And for an interesting side trip, take Route 301 north or south out of Upper Marlboro to see the tobacco barns that dot the countryside.

Travel on Route 408 through Upper Marlboro, and turn left (north) on Route 202. Then turn right on Route 556 and right again on Route 214 at Kolbes Corner. Nine miles from Upper Marlboro is a pretty wildlife preserve. Entered from the right side of the road, the preserve has auto roads, which allow you to drive past the animals from five continents that are allowed to roam freely.

Take Route 214 back to Kolbes Corner, turn right on Route 556, and then right on Route 450 to Bowie. Turn right on Belair Drive and right again on Tulip Grove Drive. There you'll find the Belair Mansion. Now used as the Bowie city offices, it once was home to two of Maryland's governors.

Follow Route 450 west through Bowie and turn right on Route 197 to Powder Mill Road. Take a left to Beltsville Research and Agricultural Center. Here research and development is done to improve the quality of plants and crops, and visitors can tour the center.

A modern point of interest is Columbia, a well-known planned community started in the late 1960s. To drive through this interesting town, continue on Powder Mill Road to Route 201. Turn right and then right again on Route 1. At the town of Laurel, turn left on Route 198 and then right on Route 29. Columbia will be on your left.

Past Columbia, continue on Route 29 to the Ellicott City turnoff. To tour this town, see details under the *National Pike*, Chapter 6. From Ellicott City, follow Frederick Road west about two miles to St. John's Church, a chapel of ease built in 1728. Return to Frederick Road and turn right on Centennial Road. Make another right on Route 40 toward the Enchanted Forest, an amusement park that will thrill the kiddies.

At this point, take Route 144 to Cookesville, about 10 miles from the Enchanted Forest. Cookesville is the site of an 1863 Civil War skirmish. Turn left on Route 97 and drive to Norbeck; turn right on Route 115. After a total of 17 miles you'll reach Rock Creek Park. The park runs along 23 miles of Rock Creek from Montgomery County to the Lincoln Memorial in the center of Washington, D.C. Rock Creek Parkway, which is not on most road maps, runs through this lovely park, providing a drive through an almost wilderness atmosphere (during the right time of day) for D.C. drivers crossing the city. For details, see Chapter 7.

From Rock Creek Park, go along Route 115 through Washington Grove and turn left on Route 124. This road will lead you to Gaithersburg, where you can visit the Bureau of Standards, if that kind of sightseeing appeals to you. If not, continue on Route 124. Keep driving straight onto Route 117 and return to Boyds to complete the circle.

Country roads

Bel Air-Churchville antique tour: about 20 miles through Harford County.

Harford County is wedged between the Pennsylvania border and the northern tip of the Chesapeake Bay. At its southeast border lies the city of Baltimore; yet the county retains a rural air and something of the Eastern Shore atmosphere, including a string of charming antique shops.

Bel Air is an antique hub in this area, with about 10 shops available for drivers on Route 22. To extend this trip, drive around the county at random or ask one of the friendly shop proprietors for directions to other county attractions.

Begin the tour on Route 1, traveling east from the Benson area. Near the intersection with Route 152, you'll find your first stop. The Antique Village is possibly the most unusual of all the antique stops, offering a look at antiques and handcrafted articles displayed in various cottages. For instance, one must-see is the leather shop, with its rich aromas and luxurious hides. Take Route 1 two or three miles east to Bel Air, the Harford County seat. Three diverse shops in the town are available for browsing. Americana Antiques, run by Carly and Ken Hill, is at 101 South Main Street. The building is full of the proprietors' collections of campy depression glass and antique furniture reproductions. In the same building is A. Miller's Rings and Things, one of the most popular "things" being a wide assortment of medicine bottles and tins. The third shop is called the Strawberry Basket. Not exactly an antique shop, the establishment is run by Donna Lowe, who does custom folk-art design and vows that she will paint anything that stands still.

Take Route 22 out of Bel Air, driving about three miles northeast to Churchville. Here you can visit six antique shops in one stop, all members of the Aldino Area Antiques Association. The six shops are open only on Monday and Tuesday.

All can be reached from Aldino Road in Churchville, and a stop at each one gives you a wide variety of antiques to choose from. The shops are Town Hall Antiques, the Time Machine, Hopkins Antiques, Hat-In-Hand, Aquilla's Attic Antiques, and the End of the Line Annex, which is in a genuine red caboose.

SOUTHERN MARYLAND (Land of Religious Tolerance)

Scenic drives

Routes 234 and 5: about 55 miles through Charles and St. Mary's counties. From Allens Fresh to Point Lookout— churches and colonial cities in the home of religious tolerance.

Southern Maryland is dominated by water and churches. The water is everywhere—in the Potomac to the south, the Chesapeake Bay to the east, and the Patuxent River to the north, and in the many tributaries, creeks, coves and inlets that carve out Maryland's irregular shoreline. The churches hold almost as much sway, with pioneer places of worship 200 years old opening their doors to parishioners of all denominations.

This tour of the area takes you on and off Routes 234 and 5 to various points of historic and scenic interest and is a good drive in any season, although spring is probably the most pleasant time of year here. Although these roads are highways, most roads through this area would be considered country roads by city dwellers, and Routes 234 and 5 are good alternatives to major highways 235 and 5, which run along the Patuxent rather than the Potomac.

Begin at the intersection of U.S. Route 301 and Route 234, near Allens Fresh. Drive about 10 miles southeast on Route 234 to Chaptico, near Route 238. There you can stop to see Christ Church, a 1736 structure built of red brick with Flemish bond. The church may have been designed by Christopher Wren.

Drive another 12 miles on Route 234 to Leonardtown, the St. Mary's County seat. In this town, Route 234 becomes Route 5.

In Leonardtown's historic district, you can visit St. Francis Xavier Church on Route 5. Built in 1766, it is the oldest standing Catholic church built in early English-speaking America. Note the bell, which was used through 1884; it is dated 1691. Next door to the church is Newtown Manor House, also worth a look. Also in Leonardtown is the Old Jail Museum, an old country "gaol" now being renovated by the county historical society. Note its original window bars and the interior features, some of which are also from the original gaol. For a further taste of the past, ask to see the old gaol records, which are available on microfilm.

From Leonardtown follow Route 245 north to Hollywood for a look at a working plantation called Sotterley—a beautiful historic site. Facing the Patuxent River, the house was built in 1717 and contains a priceless Chippendale staircase. Outside, you might see sheep grazing or take a look at the working smokehouse, where delicious hams are cured.

Return to Route 5 and take Route 249 south to Valley Lee, another spot with an interesting church. Built in 1799, Poplar Hill Church's original structure was built in 1642—at that time the first Anglican church in the state.

Return again to Route 5 and drive to St. Mary's City. This charming community was Maryland's first capital, from 1634 to 1695. Today, it is a registered national historic landmark, with many sightseeing opportunities. A mile outside the city you'll pass an outdoor altar, erected in memory of Father Andrew White, who compiled the first catechism, dictionary, and grammar in an American Indian language.

As you enter St. Mary's City, you'll be greeted by the Freedom of Conscience Monument, commemorating the religious freedom that marked young Maryland. Also in the city are St. Mary's College, founded in 1839, and the old State House, originally built in 1676 and reconstructed in 1934 for Maryland's tricentennial celebration. You can also visit Trinity Church, which is next to St. Mary's College. This ivy-covered Episcopal church was built originally in 1692. The church you see today was rebuilt from the bricks of the original state house.

Once you are beyond St. Mary's City, drive Route 5 to St.

(Above) Recent excavations at St. Mary's City uncovered a wealth of historic treasures. (Below) St. Mary's City's State House has been reconstructed for modern visitors.

1676
Reconstructed
STATE HOUSE

Inigoes. Here you'll find another church of interest. St. Inigoes, also called St. Ignatius Church, was founded in 1784 by Jesuits. The old graveyard is filled with fascinating headstones, some of Jesuits and some of very early settlers. Through the work of U.S. Navy personnel stationed at Webster Field, the church has been undergoing restoration since 1950.

The last leg of this trip takes you down Route 5 to Point Lookout, the southernmost Maryland point on the west side of the bay. At Point Lookout State Park in Scotland you can see the remains of a Civil War prison camp. There's a monument on the grounds, and camping facilities are available for overnight visitors.

Country roads

Annapolis tour: You pick the mileage through the nation's colonial capital. Annapolis, still the capital of Maryland and a popular tourist sight, really doesn't qualify as an area of country, or back, roads. Tourist crowds can be dense during peak seasons and, out of season, this is still a working-living city. If you've never seen it, however, you should at least briefly tour this quaint and beautiful town.

Late fall or winter may be your best bet for driving through Annapolis, since the number of tourists will be at a minimum. Above all, avoid Annapolis during the first week of June. This is June Week for the U.S. Naval Academy and droves of relatives and midshipmen flock the streets, celebrating graduation and participating in the week's other festivities. Hotel reservations during this week are all but impossible to get unless they have been made months in advance, so if you're planning to visit Annapolis during any part of the summer, be sure to make such arrangements before you leave home.

The first impression you get of Annapolis may be that it is a town made for tourists, rather than for year-round residents. It seems almost too perfectly preserved to be of any use to modern citizens and too picturesque to be the center of any type of action. The clue to getting more out of Annapolis than you would by taking a whirlwind tour of historic buildings is to look for the little extras that really make the city special. Overlook the obvious attractions, such as the state buildings and the naval academy, and you'll find some surprising things on your own.

Spring comes early to Annapolis. If you arrive there in late May, the roses that nearly everyone in town seems to plant are in full bloom. On May Day those roses, among other backyard garden pickings, appear in the May baskets that town residents hang from their front doors. And in the summer you can hear the strawberry man hawking his luscious wares from a little cart he wheels up and down Maryland Avenue and surrounding streets. In the fall you can watch the oystermen from the dock. If you're really lucky, one of them will sell you a dozen fresh bluepoints straight from his ship (although it's not supposed to be done).

You'll find an ethnic mixture of people in this town, all of whom offer the kind of Southern hospitality that goes along with the gardens and spic-and-span stoops that lead to the old homes. In the fall a festival is held by the town's large Greek population. And at any time of year, you're likely to find an interesting person to talk with while wandering along the dock and through the rebuilt marketplace.

This is really a beautiful town. If you want more than a glance at it, you'll have to visit on foot or on a bicycle. Keep in mind that if you're driving, the roads are rough, many of them made of the old stone or brick used for colonial roads. Consequently, speed limits are quite low and the curving roads and circles can be confusing. Pay close attention to the indications below for one-way streets to avoid tying up an already tricky traffic situation.

Start your tour at the Visitor's Gate, Gate 1, of the U.S. Naval Academy. If you want to see the academy, take a side trip inside. The grounds are large but not as attractive as the rest of the town. The academy is dominated by stark modern buildings of stone, which jar the senses when juxtaposed with the colonial town.

From Gate 1, drive north on King George Street. In the first couple of blocks you'll pass several of the more interesting homes in Annapolis. To your left will be the magnificently restored Paca House and gardens. A Visitor Center off Martin Street is your key to visiting the estate, whose gardens are one of the more spectacular sights in the city. Next you'll pass the Hammond-Harwood House, an eighteenth-century Georgian structure called by admirers "the most magnificent Georgian residence in America."

The Chase-Lloyd House at 22 Maryland Avenue was built between 1769 and 1774, and Ogle Hall at 247 King George Street was built in 1739.

At the next block, turn left on College Avenue. On your right is St. John's College, America's third oldest college. The small but pretty campus is dotted with old brick buildings. On the grounds is the famous Liberty Tree, a tulip poplar estimated to be more than 600 years old. Legend has it that the local settlers signed a peace treaty with the Susquehannock Indians under the Liberty Tree in 1652.

Two blocks west on College Avenue you'll reach Church Circle, which is one-way. Around the circle, note Reynold's Tavern, built in 1737, and St. Anne's Episcopal Church. The first church was built in the 1690s, and the present structure was built in 1858-1859.

Head off the circle onto Duke of Gloucester Street (one-way south) and drive several blocks towards the Eastport Bridge. Just before the bridge, you will pass St. Mary's Catholic Church on the right. On its grounds is the Charles Carroll of Carrollton House, not open to the public.

Turn left on Newman or St. Mary's Street to Compromise Street, and turn left (north). Pass the dock and marketplace and proceed north on Main Street (one-way). Take a right on Francis Street to State Circle, also one-way. Around State Circle you'll see the Governor's Mansion, built in 1869. Also on the circle is the Maryland Federation of Art at 19 State Circle. At 21 State Circle is the Brooksby-Shaw House, built during the eighteenth century. The Maryland State House, built between 1772 and 1779, is the oldest state house in the country still in

(Above) In the old senate chamber of Annapolis' historic State House, you can almost hear the voices of Maryland's colonial legislators. (Below) Colonial houses on Annapolis' Cornhill Street appear almost exactly as they did 200 years ago.

legislative use. Next door is the Old Treasury Building, built between 1735 and 1737.

Complete the circle and pass Francis Street again. Make a right onto Cornhill Street (one-way). The street is lined with beautifully restored homes; drive by them slowly for a close look. At the end of Cornhill Street, turn left onto Fleet Street. Here is a good example of what happens when no restoration efforts are made. Turn left again onto East Street and right back onto the circle to Maryland Avenue, which is lined with shops, a tavern, and second-floor apartments.

THE EASTERN SHORE, NORTH (Preservation Personified)

Scenic drives

Route 213 (Harmon Highway): about 55 miles through Cecil, Kent, and Queen Anne's counties. From Elkton to Centreville— traveling the pioneer path through the Eastern Shore.

The Eastern Shore of Maryland is one of the most popular sightseeing areas in the Mid-Atlantic. Offering a completely different atmosphere from its western neighbors, the Eastern Shore is full of small towns that never really grew out of their youth as fishing villages and small settlements that were based on the religious tolerance that brought the founding fathers here.

Route 213 is not scenic all the way through this drive, but where the scenery is lacking, the heritage is rich. You'll see quaint towns like Centreville and Chestertown, and you'll feel the "water aura" in the air from the rivers and inlets that formed the foundations of those early towns.

Start your tour of the upper Eastern Shore in Elkton, county seat of Cecil, which caps the bay and extends all the way to the Delaware Memorial Bridge and points northeast. If you have time to stop in Elkton, visit the Archaeological Museum of Cecil County at 135 East Main Street. I recommend a stop at the headquarters of the Historical Society of Cecil County. The building is packed with Indian artifacts found in the county and also contains an early American kitchen, a country store, and a log schoolhouse, among other attractions.

From Elkton, take Route 213 about 10 miles south to Chesapeake City on the Elk River. In South Chesapeake City you can see the Old Lock Pump House, a national historical

Old Lock Pump House on Cecil County's Chesapeake and Delaware Canal.

landmark. The pump house has a 38-foot water wheel with 12 buckets, and there's a small museum in one of its rooms.

Drive about five miles from Chesapeake City to Route 310, just north of Cayots. Off Route 213 you'll find St. Augustine Church. Built in 1838, the church was restored in 1962 and contains authentic furnishings of the era. Next to the church is the Vestry House, a log structure built in the eighteenth century and restored in 1967.

Drive five or six miles south to Warwick and Route 282. Visit Old Bohemia Church (also called St. Francis Xavier Church), built in 1704. This is one of the earliest Catholic churches built in the English colonies. Nearby is the Old Bohemia rectory, which is now a museum; old tools and farm equipment also are on display in farm buildings surrounding the church and rectory.

From Warwick, drive west on Route 282 to Earleville, where you can visit St. Stephen's Church, built in 1732. The church grounds contain the graves of some early sea captains of the area.

Return to Route 213 and drive three or four miles to Georgetown on the Sassafras River. The Kitty Knight House in this town commemorates a brave woman who is credited with dissuading a British admiral from bombarding Georgetown and neighboring Fredericktown during the War of 1812. The house now serves as an inn, a nice place to spend an overnight stay.

On the way to Chestertown, you'll pass several other churches of note. The Shrewsbury Church is located between the towns of Locust Grove and Kennedyville. Christ Church can be found between Worton and Chestertown.

When you reach Chestertown, consider taking the time to get out of your car and stretch your legs a bit. The town has many interesting sites (see *Country roads* in this section).

Cross the Chester River on Route 213 to Kingstown. Drive five or six miles to Church Hill, where you will find St. Luke's Episcopal Church. Built in 1732, this lovely church of an unusual brick tone had the misfortune to be gutted during the Civil War. The church was used as a barracks for horses and soldiers of the Federal cavalry and had to be renovated in 1881. Drive another 10 miles to Centreville and end your upper

Eastern Shore tour in this historic town (see *Country roads,* this section, for details on touring Centreville).

Country roads

A pearl of the Eastern Shore: about 10 miles through Chestertown, Kent County.

With its large group of historic sites, its riverfront, and its old-time atmosphere, Chestertown is a perfect example of pure Eastern Shore flavor. Heavily influenced by its location on the Chester and Sassafras rivers, this old town, discovered by Captain John Smith in 1608, is in Maryland's second oldest county. Chestertown really began to grow when the tobacco crops of Maryland were supplanted in importance by the timber trade and grain and other crops. But the town really came into its own during the Revolutionary War. Something of a Boston of the South, Chestertown was the most important munitions point on the Eastern Shore, and on May 23, 1774, this town with gumption held its own tea party on William Geddes' brigantine. The event is reenacted annually in Chestertown, and it is a fun event to participate in. Over the last 200 years, Chestertown also had a stint as the Eastern Shore's maritime center. Today, visitors can window shop the pleasant antique shops and observe numerous examples of the local waterfowl-carving skills. Swimming and boating are naturals for Chestertown vacationers, and hunting is a popular sport when the Canada geese migrate to the area from the north.

If you can, take a day to explore the town itself. Start the Chestertown area tour on Route 213 (Harmon Highway) near Lees Corner. Your first stop should be Washington College, the tenth oldest college in the country and the only one that George Washington honored with his name while he was alive. The campus suffered a fire in 1827, but some of the buildings date back that far. You'll find the college in Chestertown between Washington, College, and Campus avenues.

Follow Washington Avenue all the way into town and jog off onto some of the following streets to see historic homes, most of which are *not* open to the public.

This stately hall is a fine example of the attractive brick buildings on the campus of Washington College in Chestertown.

High Street

At number 102 is the Wicker House, a brick mansion with a beautiful walled garden, built in the mid-eighteenth century. Another eighteenth-century house can be seen at 109 High Street. Note its brick gable and massive chimney. At 532 High Street is the Palmer or "Rock of Ages" House. Built in the early eighteenth century, it is one-and-a-half stories tall with dormers. The fascinating thing about this house is that it is built entirely of big, angular stones that were brought to Chestertown as ship's ballast. At 414 West High Street is a two-and-a-half story brick townhouse with another huge chimney. Finally, at Front and High Streets, you'll find the Customs House, built in the early 1730s. This house was the center of the sugar trade with the British West Indies from 1730 to the mid-1780s. The Customs House also is the largest pre-Revolutionary War building still standing in the area.

Water Street

Drive east on High Street to Water Street, the riverfront road. At number 101 you'll see Widehall, a Georgian townhouse built in 1770 by the wealthiest merchant in Chestertown. At 107 is the River House, an eighteenth-century home now on the National Register of Historic Places. Built by another well-to-do merchant, it is one of Chestertown's largest merchant's mansions and was completely restored in 1971. At 109 Water Street is the former home of another merchant—a two-and-a-half story house with Flemish bond brick work, built between 1800 and 1850. At 110 Water Street is the Meteer House, a 1780 townhouse with wide chimneys, curved window arches and lots of eye-grabbing exterior detail. The last Water Street site is at 201 North Water Street, another two-and-a-half story brick building built in 1780 of Flemish bond, with cruciform chimneys.

Queen Street

Head west, away from the river, and stop at some of the following streets for sightseeing. At 105 Queen Street you'll find an old brick home built in the Queen Anne style during the second quarter of the eighteenth century. Number 111 is the Nicholson House. Built in 1788 in the Federal style, it's a good example of the late eighteenth-century merchant and tradesman houses built on this and surrounding streets, which also contain handsome early nineteenth-century houses.

Church Alley

Church Alley offers a look at the Geddes-Piper House, the only Chesapeake-Philadelphia style townhouse left standing in the area. Built in the second quarter of the eighteenth-century, the house is in the Queen Anne style, with vestigial buttresses on the four original corners. This house is the current home of the Kent County Historical Society.

Park Row

On Cross Street and Park Row, you will see Emmanuel Protestant Episcopal Church, a redecorated colonial style building erected in 1772. At Park and Lawyer's rows you'll find the Masonic Building, built in 1827 in three sections, in the late Federal period style.

Mill Street

At 101-103 South Mill Street is one of Chestertown's most interesting buildings. This three-section frame "telescope" structure is the last of its kind in Chestertown. Built in the mid-to-late eighteenth century, the house contains two separate residences, with gorgeous gardens in the rear. At 107 South Mill Street is a house called Sterling Castle, although it is only one-and-a-half stories tall—a frame, dormered eighteenth-century house.

St. Paul's Episcopal Church. Built in 1713, this is the oldest continually used Episcopal church in Maryland. Legend has it that it cost 70,000 pounds of tobacco to build. The adjacent vestry house was built in 1766 and the trees in the churchyard have been there since the pre-colonial days.

Take Route 20 south, about ten minutes' drive south of Chestertown, to Remington Farms. This is 3,000 acres of land devoted to wildlife research and demonstration. On the grounds are woods, marshland, and ponds. Nature trails wind through the preserve, and from October to May you can spot the wintering Canada and snow geese.

Continue on Route 20 to the waterfront village of Rock Hall, about 12 miles south of Chestertown. This fishing village is worth a visit, if for no other reason than to watch the operations of clam, crab, oyster, and fish processing.

Drive to the intersection of Routes 20 and 445 and take Route 445 south to Eastern Neck National Wildlife Refuge. The scenery is composed of the bay and unspoiled woodlands. Visitors can rent boats to continue their tour out to the bay waters.

Touring Wye Territory: about 20 miles through Queen Anne's and Talbot counties.

Centreville and its Talbot County neighbor, Wye Mills, form an interesting tour at the eastern end of the Chesapeake Bay Bridge. Named after the queen of Great Britain, Queen Anne's County drew some of its first settlers from other colonies who were seeking religious freedom through the Maryland Toleration Act of 1649. Centreville itself was formed as these pioneers gravitated toward the navigable tributaries of the Chesapeake Bay, and today you can see remnants of those early settlements.

Historic Centreville, Queen Anne's County, has this statue of Queen Anne of Great Britain in the town's center

Head for Centreville on Route 301 or Route 213. In Centreville, take Commerce Street to the county courthouse. The 1792 courthouse is the oldest Maryland County courthouse in continuous use. Next to it is Lawyer's Row, where a group of restored eighteenth-century buildings are now used as offices. At 120 South Commerce Street is the Tucker House, an eighteenth-century building now housing the county historical society. At 119 South Commerce Street is Wright's Chance, a small manor house built in 1744. The house, part of an old plantation patented in 1681, was moved from four miles out of town to this site in 1964. Note the old glass in its windows.

Leave Centreville via Route 213 south and drive to Wye Mills in Talbot County, off Route 662. There you will find the 1721 Wye Church, one of the oldest American Episcopal churches, restored in 1949. You'll also have a chance to look at the Wye Oak, Maryland's state tree. In the middle of a small state park, the tree is the largest white oak in the state. It is 95 feet tall, with a horizontal span of 165 feet and a trunk whose circumference is 21 feet. It is thought to be more than 400 years old. Near the tree, you can explore an early American schoolroom. Wye Mills was named for the mill on this site, which ground flour for Washington's troops at Valley Forge in 1778. In continual operation since 1760, this mill has been restored for limited operation and produces terrific water-ground cornmeal, which you can purchase.

This lovely brick church—Wye Church—is another attraction in Talbot County's Wye Mills.

Wye Oak, said to be more than four hundred years old, is one of the many sights in Wye Mills, Talbot County.

Twentieth-century mill workers grind flour at famous Wye Mill.

Take Route 662 north to Route 50 west and drive to Carmichael Road. Drive south on Carmichael Road five miles to the Wye Angus Visitors Center at Wye Plantation. This is the home of the famous black Angus herd raised through "genetic breeding reinforced by natural living conditions." The natural living conditions consist of a four-mile peninsula surrounded and separated from the mainland by branches of the Wye River. The land was a farm during the seventeenth century, and the Angus herd was started here in 1938.

From the plantation, take Route 50 west to Kent Narrows Bridge. Before crossing the drawbridge, consider driving off the road into the interesting narrows area. If you wind through the roads in the narrows, you'll see swaying marsh grasses, lively marinas, and two good seafood restaurants. You'll also be able to watch the fishing, crabbing, clamming, and oystering operations of local watermen. For more information on this area, head for the Information Center, reached from the first right turn after the bridge, *eastbound* on Route 50.

For a tourist weekend of historic sightseeing, cross the bay bridge west to Annapolis (see *Country roads, Southern Maryland, page 34*).

Denton-Area antique tour: about 30 miles through Caroline County.

Like most Eastern Shore locales, Caroline County, around Denton, offers antique buffs a wealth of shops. Starting in Hillsboro at Routes 404 and 480, you'll find Jean Cooper's Country Shop about eight miles west of Denton. Antique decoys, marbletop furniture, and lots of hanging planters are for sale here.

Drive 12 miles east on Route 404. About four miles east of Denton is the Country Store. Truly an old country store, this shop is really packed with junk and antiques, giving you lots of things to choose from.

Turn right (south) on Route 313 and drive about 10 miles to Federalsburg. There you'll find Henry's New and Used Furniture on Walkerton Road. Henry recently acquired an extra shop north of this location and now has room to show the antiques he has collected and stored over the years, in addition to his selection of new furniture.

From Federalsburg, drive west on Route 318 about seven miles to Preston, which has two shops. First is Ye Olde Post Shop on Main Street. This former post office building has few antiques, specializing rather in craft items, such as needlework and hand-made candles. One block away on Main Street is Henry Etta McMahon's Ye Quaker Bonnet. This unusual shop is in two side-by-side buildings—a former tavern and a funeral parlor. The charming proprietor will make your visit a lot of fun, and the kids will be especially enamored of a gigantic dollhouse in the shop.

From Preston, take Route 16 north about five miles and turn right on Route 621. After about three miles you'll reach American Corners, where you can visit Curtis Andrew's Auction Barn. This is a great place, and if you are in the vicinity on a Thursday, stop for the Thursday night auctions held in the barn. Visitors are allowed to inspect the barn's antiques and used furniture before the auction.

EASTERN SHORE, SOUTH (Maryland's Outback)

Scenic drives

Circle tour: about 110 miles through Worcester, Somerset, and Wicomico counties. From the Pocomoke to the Wicomico— cypress swamps, loblolly pine forests, iron furnaces, seafood, and a haunted church.

The lower Eastern Shore sometimes is called Maryland's outback. Tucked in between Delaware and Virginia, between the Chesapeake and the Atlantic, this wild territory offers natural views found nowhere else in the state. Along with the scenery come some really unique points of interest, including more old, old churches and a few communities that seem to have been frozen in time.

This tour can be done at any time of year, although spring or summer might be the most pleasant and the most colorful. Take your time on this tour; you might want to plan an overnight stay somewhere along the line. This area also provides entry points to other Mid-Atlantic tours. To the east is the famous Assateague Island, and to the north is Delaware's seashore drive, possibly the only really scenic part of that state. For an even longer drive, you can head northwest from the lower Eastern Shore to the upper Eastern Shore and points west.

Start the tour in the northeast corner of Worcester County on Route 113, west of the intersection with Route 589. Here you'll find Old St. Martin's Church, one of the most intriguing sights on the tour and a fitting place to begin. Built in 1756 of colonial brick, the first church building was built in 1700 as the original Protestant Episcopal Church of Worcester County. The neat thing about this mysterious church is that locals say it is haunted! As legend has it, a veiled maiden is wont to glide eerily through the church and across the road, only to fade into the marshes. And an antique gold collection plate that belongs to the church has been said to glide along the pews all by itself, clanking as ghostly coins drops into it. Enter if you dare!

From the church, take Route 113 south about five miles to Berlin. Berlin offers the Stephen Decatur Memorial. The War of 1812 hero, famous for saying, "My country—may she ever be right, but right or wrong, my country!" was born in a small house that used to be across the street from the memorial. While you are visiting, you can use the adjacent park for a picnic.

Continue about 15 miles south on Route 113, past Ironshire, Newark, and Basket Switch to the town of Snow Hill. At this point you are entering the Pocomoke River Area. Chartered in 1686, the town became a port of entry in 1694 and the tiny village retains its colonial aura. One of the places to stop at in town is the Julia A. Purnell Museum at 204 West Main Street. This museum should not be missed. Adults and children alike will revel in the assortment of oddities and colonial household items. Included in the fascinating array are a harp that belonged to General Tom Thumb, along with his bathtub and dressed fleas. On the grisly side, you can also see John Wilkes Booth's assassination weapon. There's also an unfamiliar array of nonelectric appliances that would chill the bones of today's home-maker.

Also in Snow Hill is All Hallows Episcopal Church at Church and Market streets. This 1748 church is built of beautiful brick; inside are several items of interest. There's a 1701 Bible and a bell that hangs between two cedar trees out front. Both were gifts to the church from Queen Anne.

A good side trip may be taken by turning right (north) on Route 12 at the traffic light in town, and driving four miles to Old Furnace Road. Turn left there to Nassawango Furnace. This 1830s structure, once used for smelting iron ore taken from the Pocomoke Forest swamps, is now being restored.

Returning from the side trip, you will find Pocomoke State Forest to the south. It contains 12,000 acres of land between Snow Hill and Pocomoke City, all filled with loblolly pine. The almost spooky Pocomoke River is deep and dark. It looks more like a tropical river than the type of river you would expect to find in Maryland. Water lilies float along the water; bald cypress trees thrive in the swamp bordering the river. This is one of the most significant stands of bald cypress this far north. The Pocomoke is a strange mixture of saltwater, freshwater, and brackish water. It is filled with good fishing opportunities—rockfish, largemouth bass, and crappies are among the species to be caught.

About four-and-a-half miles south of Snow Hill is the forest's Shad Landing State Park on the river. This dense forest used to be a perfect hiding place for ships carrying contraband. It lies along the route that was used by the Underground Railroad in leading slaves to freedom in the north. At the park you can stop to camp, fish, swim in the pool, picnic, or go boating.

About four miles farther south, outside of Pocomoke City, you'll find Millburn Landing State Park, which offers attractions and facilities similar to those at Shad Landing.

Pass through Pocomoke City and take Route 13 to Route 667. Turn left on Route 406 and drive to Rehobeth (11 miles from Pocomoke City). This tiny village has two historic churches. The Rehobeth Presbyterian Church, built in 1706, is the oldest Presbyterian Church in the United States. All that is left of the Coventry Episcopal Church, built in 1740, is ruins, but you might want to check it out anyway.

Follow Route 667 about 11 miles farther to St. Peter's Methodist Church. To find the church, take a right onto Thomas Long Road. Founded in 1782, the present church was built around 1850, and there preached Joshua Thomas, called the "Parson of the Island."

Take Routes 667 and 413 south about three miles to Crisfield, often called the "Seafood Capital of the World." Overlooking Chesapeake Bay, this town offers a look at the old skipjacks still used for oystering. An interesting side trip can be made via a 10-minute ferry ride from the city dock to Smith Island. A man named West bought the island in 1666 for two overcoats. Today the island is completely involved in the seafood industry. The ferry leaves daily at 12:30 and 3:00 P.M.

Stop in Crisfield, Somerset County, to see the annual Crab Derby held during the summer.

Drive along Route 413 north about 20 miles to Princess Anne, the Somerset county seat. Founded in 1666 and incorporated in 1733, the town is full of historic points of interest. There are vestiges of the late seventeenth century, but most of the buildings you see today were built in the late eighteenth century. They include the Teackle Mansion, St. Andrew's Episcopal Church, the Boxwood Gardens, Washington Hotel, Manokin Presbyterian Church, and Tunstall Cottage. See as many of these as time and desire permit.

From Princess Anne, take Route 13 north to Salisbury, about a 12-mile drive. Salisbury is the largest city on the lower Eastern Shore and probably always has been the largest since it was founded. Originally called Handy's Landing, the town was formed where several Indian trails converged at the Wicomico River. Unfortunately, most of the town's colonial buildings were

The Teackle Mansion is one of many historic sites to visit in the town of Princess Anne.

destroyed in a fire, so it's probably best not to stop, but to drive straight through.

From Salisbury, take Route 346 east to Pittsville, about a 10-mile drive. Turn right on Route 353 and drive two miles to Wicomico State Forest. The 1,100-acre forest is filled with the local loblolly pines and is the site of botanical research concerning that species.

From the forest, turn left on Route 350 to Route 374 and cross Pocomoke Road. You can return on Route 374 to Berlin to complete the circle.

Ocean City Drive: see *Ocean Drive, Delaware,* page 000.

Country roads

Eastern Shore river tour: about 45 miles through Dorchester County.

Dorchester County is beautiful. Large areas of the county could be considered wilderness. The first settlers in this land used its rivers as their highways—the Choptank, Little Choptank, Honga, and Blackwater rivers crisscross over the relatively flat land. There is a variety of sights for drivers, some natural and some historic. Possibly the best feature is Blackwater National Wildlife Refuge, wintering grounds for huge flocks of Canada geese. With this in mind, this tour is probably best taken in late fall or winter, when you can see the geese.

Start your tour of Dorchester County at the town of James, on Route 343. Drive three miles east to Cornersville and a couple of miles to restored Spocott Windmill in Lloyds (six miles from Cambridge). Around the year 1850 the original Spocott windmill was built on these grounds. One of 18 post windmills built in colonial Dorchester County, it was destroyed, and the one you see today was reconstructed in 1971 from the original specifications. This copy is the only post windmill left in the area, since the last of the original 18 was destroyed in a recent hurricane. Also on the grounds is a miller's house, built between 1775 and 1840, restored, and moved to the site of the new windmill.

Proceed to Cambridge, an old port town founded in 1684. Now a seafood center thriving on that light industry, the town and its outskirts offer several stops. Just before you reach the town, turn left onto Horns Point Road to visit the Dorchester Heritage Museum. Open on weekends, it contains displays of county history.

Among the many historic sites in town is Christ P.E. Church on High Street. The church was built in 1883; its graveyard is much older. Two of the gravestones are dated 1678 and 1684; others mark the resting places of five Maryland governors from Dorchester County, along with those of Revolutionary War heroes and other notables of the past. On LaGrange Avenue you will find the Meredith House and Farm Museum. The historical society of the county resides in the building, which dates back to 1760. There is a governor's room honoring those five Dorchester governors. Outbuildings include a blacksmith shop, a building with old farm tools, and a smokehouse.

From Cambridge, take Route 50 to Route 16 west (a right turn). About two miles past Church Creek, you'll reach Old Trinity Episcopal Church. Built in 1675, the small, well-restored brick church is the oldest Protestant church in the country still in use. It's open every day except Tuesday. You'll notice the graves of some famous former residents—members of the Carroll family among them. Be sure to check out the unusual miller's grave there, marked with old millstones.

Continue west on Route 16 to Woolford, about a mile west to the Old School Baptist Meeting House, built in 1790—a small white wooden building.

Drive about eight miles to Taylor's Island. There you'll find an interesting chapel of ease connected with the Mission of Old Trinity Church. Erected in 1707 to save area settlers a nine-mile trip to the main church, it has been restored and has a rich history. It was once used as a school and once as a blacksmith's shop.

Backtrack to Route 335 south (a right turn) and drive to Church Creek. On the left side of the road is a one-room schoolhouse. The building is now being restored and there are plans to turn it into a museum; it is thought to have sheltered troops during the Civil War.

Blackwater National Wildlife Refuge offers a look at migrating Canada geese during late fall and winter.

Turn left on Key Wallace Drive to reach the 12,000-acre Blackwater National Wildlife Refuge. A Visitor Center is on the right. If you do take the tour during late fall or winter, you can see some of the 100,000 wintering Canada geese. At any other time of year you might spot a bald eagle, rare Delmarva fox squirrel, white-tail deer, some muskrat, nutria, turtles, and woodpeckers. Keep in mind that the Visitor Center is closed during June, July, and August.

From the wildlife refuge, continue on Route 335, bearing right and curving around the Honga River. Near Golden Hill, you'll find yet another significant church, St. Mary's Star of the Sea, founded in 1769, the first Catholic chapel in the county. The 1872 church has been used in the past as a schoolhouse and is now being restored.

Drive about five miles to Honga on Hooper Island. This quaint, bridge-connected island group was settled by the Hooper family in the mid-1600s and offers delicious seafood to modern visitors. Finish your tour at Hoopersville or Richland Point on the island.

Visiting the wild ponies: 30 to 40 miles along Assateague Island, Worcester County.

Assateague Island is famous nationally for the unusual ponies that roam freely there. Called Assateague or Chincoteague ponies, these sturdy little creatures are thought to have been let onto the island to graze by seventeenth-century settlers from the mainland. The theory is that some of the ponies were never retrieved and a breed that could survive mainly on marsh grasses and bayberry leaves developed over a period of 300 years. Assateague Island comes under the jurisdiction of both Maryland and Virginia. Today there is a herd of the ponies at each end of the island.

Besides the ponies, Assateague offers the usual beachside recreation—swimming, crabbing, fishing, boating, camping, etc. The most important thing to keep in mind about the island is that if you want to see the more isolated sections, you'll have to hike or drive an oversand vehicle. Oversand vehicles are those with four-wheel drive. In order to get a beach-access permit, the vehicle also must carry a shovel, tire gauge, jack and support, and tow ropes or a chain. So make your preparations in advance to get the best out of this island trip.

The island is divided into four main sections, north to south. One small section in the north will remain private until 1980. The others are (north to south): Assateague State Park (Maryland), Assateague Island National Seashore, Chincoteague National Wildlife Refuge, and another Assateague Island National Seashore section.

To reach the island, take Maryland Route 611. To reach Route 611, take U.S. Route 113 to Route 376 east, turn right onto Route 611, and cross the bay to the state park end of the island. There is a place for area parking, an information center, and campground registration. Drive about two miles south to North Beach Drive in the national seashore section, where you'll find a beach, a canoe launch on the bay, crabbing, hiking, surf fishing, camping, and more parking space.

Drive another mile or two to the end of the paved drive. A 14-mile back trail starts here—for hikers and oversand vehicles with permits *only*. At the Maryland-Virginia state line, you enter

Chincoteague National Wildlife Refuge, 12 miles of wild beach accessible only on foot. At the south end of the wildlife refuge is a wildlife drive to be used by hikers and cyclists until 3:00 P.M. and open to cars from 3:00 P.M. to dark. This route can be reached by getting onto the island from Chincoteague, Virginia. There is another information center here, an auditorium, and a Coast Guard lighthouse.

Bear right (south) to Beach Road on the national seashore section in Virginia. Here is another Visitor Center, as well as parking lots, beach, picnic areas, and an outdoor amphitheater. To investigate this part of the island, drive Toms Cove Road about two-and-a-half miles to its end. Here is the beginning of another oversand route, about three miles long, that takes you to the island's hooked southern tip, Fishing Point.

3

New Jersey

NORTHERN NEW JERSEY (Metropolis to Wilderness)

Scenic drives

Old Mine Road: about 50 miles through Sussex and Warren counties. From Delaware Water Gap to High Point State Park—New Jersey's mountain country and the Delaware River.

Shared by Pennsylvania and New Jersey, the Delaware Water Gap is one of the Mid-Atlantic's most intriguing natural landmarks. In fact, some admirers call this area the most beautiful in all of New Jersey. The awesome mountain gap that makes way for the mighty Delaware River has attracted vacationers and sightseers for more than a century, and rightfully so. The air is invigorating, the panoramas are breathtaking in any season, and the gap is within easy driving distance of both Philadelphia and New York City. Today's visitors may even see some of the same resorts that served as summer havens for the wealthy city dwellers of the nineteenth century.

The twentieth century has brought new attractions to the gap, where you'll find a pleasant mix of the old and the new. Since 1966 the National Park Service has been acquiring land for the Delaware Water Gap National Recreation Area, planned for a total of 70,000 acres. A lot of the land is still in private ownership, but canoeing, ice fishing, swimming, ice skating, snowmobiling, hiking and nature walks are available to current visitors. And if you have time to sightsee, there are several unusual communities in the vicinity.

A clear autumn day is probably the best time to drive Old Mine Road, with the fall colors particularly spectacular in the Kittatinny Mountains. Summertime also is lovely, but it will bring extra auto traffic. Before the white settlers arrived, these mountains were home to the Lenni Lenape Indians, said to have been the most peaceful of all the Northeastern tribes. In relatively peaceful encounters, the Lenni Lenape were driven northward, where the small tribe was quickly overwhelmed by its more warlike brothers. Today, the Lenni Lenape are a lost people of a lost age. Only their spirits remain in the land they once called home. Perhaps it is these spirits that lend modern visitors the peace of mind the very mountains seem to exude.

Old Mine Road runs through the entire recreation area, from High Point State Park in New Jersey's northwest corner to the gap itself. Most of the back roads in the area are poorly marked and can be quite confusing. If you don't intend to make any side trips, your best bet is to try to keep the river in view. If you decide to detour, however, keep track of landmarks and pay attention to road signs.

Many travelers prefer to see this area by driving half the route through New Jersey and half through Pennsylvania. For details on the Pennsylvania banks of the Delaware, see Chapter 5, page 122.

The tour along Old Mine Road is only about 50 miles, but if you want to make a day of it, begin at the gap. Off Interstate Route 80 is Kittatinny Point Information Station, where you can pick up brochures on sights and history of the area. The information center is closed during the winter, so if you're driving then, start at the park headquarters, south of the information station. At either site friendly staff members will give you helpful directions.

To get a true feel for the gap—especially if you're a freak for heights—begin your tour with a stop at all three of the gap overlooks on the Pennsylvania side, off Route 611. The first is at Arrow Island, a few miles south of Delaware Water Gap. If you're heading north, the next overlook is at Point of Gap, and the third is at Resort Point at the gap. If you don't feel like crossing the bridge into Pennsylvania, you can check the view from New Jersey's Kittatinny Overlook at the information station.

From any of these points, you can watch the water— sometimes 90 feet deep—ooze through the narrow slot as the banks squeeze together and rise sharply to the mountains. For hikers, the famed Appalachian Trail runs through the gap and northward, parallel to the river.

About a mile north of the gap you can stop again at the Fairview parking area. The next stretch of the river is divided by two large islands and two smaller ones—Shawnee and DePue islands, followed by Labar and Tocks islands. Just south of Tocks Island the park service plans to construct a dam and impoundments to form a large reservoir on the river.

Past Tocks Island you enter the Worthington State Forest region. As you proceed northward, you'll spot pretty lakes to the east. Many of them are manmade, like the lake at Watergate, which offers excellent fishing. Hiking trails from Watergate lead into the forests of Kittatinny Mountain, making this a good launching point for outdoor pursuits. Local residents are very friendly, and on summer weekends you can stop to hear outdoor concerts at the Watergate bandshell. During the winter there are ice skating and ice fishing.

Just north of Watergate is the town of Millbrook, and if you're there in summertime, be sure to stop. This quaint community started as little more than a grist mill, a brook (the one that gave it its name), and a few farms. Going the way of many ambitious young communities of the nineteenth century, Millbrook was overshadowed by the larger metropolises nearby, leaving it destined for obscurity. Today the residents are recreating the thriving village that Millbrook was during the late 1800s. Residents are making donations of antique furniture and giving their own time to the restoration effort. If you drive by there between July and Labor Day, you can explore the hotel, blacksmith shop, church, schoolhouse, weaving shop, shoemaker's shop, and several residences.

Next, you'll reach the S-curve in the river called Wallpack Bend. From there you can visit the Artists for Environment Program sponsored by the National Park Service with several Eastern art schools. Look for the white house on the hillside overlooking the bend. You're likely to find at least one artist on the hillside, painting the scene.

From the bend you'll enter Flatbrook Valley, with its creek and the town of Flatbrookville. Past the town and just south of Wallpack Center is Buttermilk Falls. This beautiful rush of water drains off the Kittatinny range's Rattlesnake Mountain into the valley below. Once cleared and farmed, that low land has been retaken by Mother Nature and is covered in spring by pink and white rhododendron blossoms. To explore this scenic area on foot, take one of the hiking trails that emanate from the falls.

North of Wallpack Center is Thunder Mountain Vocational-Environmental Education Center, another park service project sponsored in conjunction with the New Jersey Department of Education and the Newton School District. The former dude ranch is now a working demonstration farm where urbanites can get back to the land, at least momentarily. Open weekdays, except during December, the farm is sometimes crowded with visiting youth groups.

Farther north lies Peters Valley Craft Village, another area town that has undergone a recent metamorphosis. Once just a small farm community during the nineteenth century, Peters Valley is now a town of many skilled artisans, dedicated to preserving the manual skills of early America. Between April and December travelers can visit the studios of local wood-carvers and woodworkers, weavers, blacksmiths, ceramics craftsmen, and jewelry makers. Keep in mind, though, that the studios are closed during the morning and on Mondays. If your timing is right, you'll hit the annual craft fair—two summer days of booths and festivities that demonstrate the community's purpose.

Stay on Old Mine Road north from Peters Valley or take Route 206 east to Stokes State Forest, another pretty drive. If you decide to include Pennsylvania in your tour, you can take the toll bridge at Dingman's Ferry or at Milford. If you stay in New Jersey, you'll end up in High Point State Park, where the elevation is 1,803 feet.

Country roads

Morristown National Historical Park: five to ten miles through Morris County. From 1777 to 1780—following the trail of the Continental Army through the Revolutionary War.

The Garden State usually brings to mind visions of concrete and steel rather than soil and fruit. New Jersey also is called the corridor state because some consider it little more than the connection between New York and Philadelphia. Endless jokes are cracked about Newark, and Easterners have moaned and groaned for years about the infamous "green stamp," as truckers call the boring turnpike. To top it off, northern New Jersey, the northeast in particular, is avoided by pursuers of panorama the way their Midwestern comrades avoid Gary, Indiana.

Often shunned by tourists and long-distance travelers, northeast New Jersey deserves a visit if for no other reason than to learn of its significant role in the formation of the Union and in the Revolutionary War in particular. During two harrowing winters Morristown sheltered the main encampment of the Continental Army led by George Washington. New Jersey saw a lot of action during the war, and Morristown was a particularly strategic location for the army. To the east, the timeworn Watchung Mountains helped the bedraggled troops confine the British in New York, while they reinforced their ranks in New Jersey.

Via Route 202, this not-quite-scenic tour takes you along the route that Washington's army marched. Although Morristown, like most of the towns in this region, has succumbed to the architectural developments of our age, try to ignore the modern structures and visualize the struggling army and the events that took place here.

As you enter the town, Morristown Green will be on your left. When George Washington led his troops into Morristown for the winter of '77, the green was full of grazing farm animals and the surrounding buildings consisted of two churches and a few other scattered structures. The soldiers were put up in every shelter from farmhouse to barn and storehouse. Although the winter was hard, the army succeeded in reinforcing its strength during its 1777 stay, moving north to confront the British in the spring of 1778.

Two years later the army returned. Its stay over the winter of 1779-80 proved almost fatal to the Continental Army, as well as to independence efforts. Many thousands of soldiers succumbed to disease, starvation, and the mutinies of desperate men.

Circle the Morristown Green by turning left onto Route 24 from Route 202, and go left again onto Morris Avenue East (Route 510), past the exit ramp from Route 287. Turn left onto Morris Avenue West, and watch for the parking lot at Washington's Headquarters. In this park is the house of Colonel Jacob Ford, Jr., and his family, where Washington and his staff officers stayed during the 1779-80 winter.

From the park, turn left onto Morris Avenue West, which runs into Morris Avenue East. Turn right onto Route 24 and left onto Western Avenue. At Ann Street, turn left again.

From Ann Street, turn right into Fort Nonsense, so-named because rumor has it that Washington ordered its 1777 construction for no other reason than to keep the troops busy—digging trenches and raised embankments.

From Fort Nonsense, drive back onto Western (a left turn from Ann Street). Past Bailey Hollow Road is Morristown National Historical Park, with a parking lot off the right side of the street. For a view of the park, continue south on Western Avenue to Jockey Hollow Road. There you'll find a Visitor Center and parking lot at the park road off Tempe Wick Road. The Jockey Hollow Encampment area is the spot where Washington's army built 1,000 huts in 1779. To the north, on Sugar Loaf Road, is the Wick Farm. General Arthur St. Clair had his headquarters here during the 1779-80 winter. The Wicks' home was atypical of area farmhouses, being much more lavish than most of the modest abodes of the period.

Next on Sugar Loaf Road is Sugar Loaf Hill, where 2,000 soldiers waited out the winter in crude hillside huts. Turn right before the Pennsylvania Line parking lot nearby to see the Grand Parade, where those valiant soldiers went through the drills, marches, inspection, guard assignments, and discipline that made up their daily routine. Circle to the left, around Western Avenue, and head toward Lewis Morris County Park. At the Sugar Loaf parking area, you'll find overlooks, parking areas, and picnic spots to complete your Morristown tour.

In and around the suburbs: About 10 miles through historic Union County.

U.S. Route 22 runs east to west through one of the most densely populated sections of New Jersey. Needless to say, the road is not a scenic drive, nor is it a country road. Route 22 is the major artery connecting the Union County towns west of Elizabeth. The shopping centers that line it draw lots of traffic to the road. Union County does deserve some attention, however, if only to show out-of-towners what is beneath the sometimes unattractive surface.

If you look carefully among the commercial and residential structures and the crisscrossing ribbons of highways, you're likely to find some interesting historic sites besides enjoying a pleasant drive or two through the suburbs. Extensive development has left the county with no roads worth driving from end to end, but the area is full of gently rolling hills and old houses. Your best bet for a Sunday afternoon drive is to proceed east to west on Route 22, bearing north off the highway when the spirit hits you. Make the drive during the fall, when the brilliant colors overshadow the grays of manmade steel and concrete.

If you live in the area or if you're traveling through and cannot avoid Route 22, try stopping at some of the following sites. All are directly off Route 22, making it easy to return to the highway for the rest of your trip.

The first town to stop at is Union. Driving westward, turn right onto Stuyvesant Avenue. You'll find Connecticut Farms Church at 892 Stuyvesant Avenue. The original church on this site was built in 1740 and burned by the British some years later. Rebuilt in 1783, the simple church welcomes modern visitors.

The Bonnel Homestead, now housing Bonnel Antiques, is at 883 West Chestnut Street. It can be reached by making the same turn onto Stuyvesant Avenue and then bearing left immediately. Built in 1797, the structure was the farmhouse of Nathaniel Bonnel, former sheriff of Union County.

Back on Route 22, drive about five miles west to the town of Westfield. There you'll find the famous Miller-Cory House, built in 1740. Turn left onto Mountain Avenue; the house and museum are at number 614. This fascinating site is known as a living museum, where Sunday afternoon visitors can observe the workings of eighteenth-century farm life, including a utility and dye garden, the "necessary," the main house, a corncrib, an education center, an orchard, and a storeroom. Miller and Cory were two of the pre-Revolutionary War owners of the house.

Just east of Westfield is the town of Scotch Plains. From Route 22 make a left turn onto Park Avenue. At the corner of Park Avenue and Front Street is the Stage House Inn and Village, an interesting group of eighteenth-century buildings that have been preserved and are now used as shops. You can investigate the buildings during regular business hours or by appointment. Whatever you have time for, be sure to see the Greek Revival outhouse that Duncan Phyfe built for his daughter.

CENTRAL NEW JERSEY (The Pine Barrens)

Scenic drives

Routes 519 and 29: about 60 miles through Warren, Hunterdon, and Mercer counties. From Belvidere to Trenton—following the Delaware River from the gap.

This tour is a continuation of the Delaware Water Gap-Kittatinny Mountains trip, picking up the river at Belvidere and running through mountain and stream country to the state capital. Belvidere can be found on the New Jersey-Pennsylvania border, a mile or two south of Route 46. From Belvidere, take Route 519 south, beginning your trip with a cruise between

Marble and Scott mountains. Drive a little more than 10 miles to Route 57, around Phillipsburg. Follow the signs for Route 519 south.

Ten miles south of Phillipsburg, Route 519 runs by Musconetcong Mountain and on to Milford, on the river. Continue to Frenchtown and take Route 29 south. From here to Trenton the route runs parallel with the Delaware River; you leave the mountain territory. One of the main features in the flatter land is the tributaries of the Delaware. Several state parks along the way offer camping on both the New Jersey and the Pennsylvania sides of the river.

The first camping area is at Raven Rock about 10 miles south of Frenchtown. Drive another 10 miles to the Lambertville (New Jersey)-New Hope (Pennsylvania) area. On the Pennsylvania side you'll find Roosevelt State Historic Park, but no camping is allowed there.

For camping, drive about six miles south to Titusville. Washington Crossing State Park offers camping there, and there's a monument to visit on the Pennsylvania side. The park is about 10 miles away from Trenton; it makes a good stopping point for the trip.

Country roads

Tuckerton Road: 35 miles through Ocean, Burlington, and Camden counties. From Tuckerton to Berlin—exploring the Pine Barrens via the old Philadelphia-Tuckerton stagecoach run.

The Pine Barrens might be considered New Jersey's forgotten territory. Totalling more than a million acres, it is a lot of land to dismiss, especially in a state that houses 50,000 people per square mile in some places. But in the Pines you'll find only about 15 people per square mile—if you can find any at all.

When the settlers first discovered this area of sand, bogs, and pine trees, they gave it the name of "Barrens" because it was impossible to farm. Most settlers pushed on to more fertile land. Today the pines come as a surprise to residents of nearby cities, who are usually completely unaware of the wilderness that sits

smack-dab in the center of the megalopolis stretching from
Boston to Richmond. The Pine Barrens offer a quiet kind of
beauty, rising more from the untouched quality of the land than
from any awesome natural landmark.

The central Pine Barrens cover 650,000 acres. Newcomers to
the area always ask this incredulous question first: "How far
does this forest go?" Well, it covers about 1,000 square miles.
Trying to see the whole territory could take days. You could get
hopelessly lost if you wander at random. Most of the roads
through this forest are two-track sand roads, many blazed
during the pioneer days. The people you'll find here are likely to
be descended from the Revolutionary War era families that tried
to tame this land.

The best way to see the Pine Barrens is to drive one of these
sand roads, stopping along the way to climb a hill to one of the
forest's numerous fire towers. From the towers, forest stretches
below you as far as the eye can see. There are 20 types of native
orchids, plus deer, otter, raccoon, gray fox, and mink. And there
are swarms of the dread New Jersey mosquito. You'll pass
narrow rivers, bogs coated with cranberries and, in the plains,
the mysterious dwarf pines that grow to only a fraction of their
normal height.

If all that doesn't interest you, go just to meet some of the
people of the barrens, locally called "pineys." Many of these
rugged individuals still make a living off the woods, as did their
forefathers. During the nineteenth century, bog iron was discovered in the barrens, providing income for area residents. But
when iron and coal were found to the west in Pennsylvania, the
pineys were left to find a new livelihood, and many of them
turned to making paper and glass. Alas, at the advent of the
twentieth century, such industry moved to the cities, leaving the
pineys in the lurch once again. As a consequence, many thriving
towns in the pines disappeared, leaving only traces of these lively
communities. Today's pineys depend more and more on surrounding urban areas for their income, but a few diehards still
live completely off the land. In the winter charcoal can be made;
in the spring they pull sphagnum moss from the bogs to sell to
florists; in the summer they knock wild blueberries into baskets

hung from their necks; and in the fall they gather cranberries. Around Christmastime the local pine cones (called pineballs in the area) are also in demand, and some locals gather cattails during the summer.

One of the first things you might notice about the pineys you meet is that many of them look younger than they are—perhaps it's the air. Longtime residents are fiercely loyal to the pines area, declaring they wouldn't live anywhere else. A recent conservation move has emerged, attempting to deter developers from taking over the wilderness. You can protect the wilderness yourself by not leaving trash behind you and by treading softly. It is especially important to follow Smokey the Bear's advice here: the Pine Barrens suffer many fires each year, so be extremely careful with matches and cigarettes. Thousands of acres can be devastated in a matter of hours.

The wet areas of the pines are truly fascinating. You'll pass mysterious bogs with their carnivorous plants, beautiful narrow rivers, and the unique areas called spongs and cripples. A spong is a low wet area; a cripple is a spong in which white cedars grow.

The sand roads through the barrens are extremely confusing to outsiders, although locals often know them well enough to travel blindfolded through the pines. If you should decide to explore, it's a good idea to check with local residents for directions and tips on road conditions. For the following drive, in fact, it's best to have a vehicle with four-wheel drive. If you want to avoid this kind of driving, follow one of the paved routes listed at the end of this section.

Start in the town of Tuckerton, about two miles inland of Little Egg Harbor. Be sure to ask for directions and get an update on Tuckerton Road conditions before setting out. The Tuckerton Road, a former stagecoach route, remains much the same as it was when the towns along it lived and offers a great view of the pines. It may have been the first dual highway in the country—since traffic was so heavy on it during its prime that it became two-lane in certain stretches. As you drive west along the sand road, try to picture the taverns that lined it, selling such exotic drinks as metheglin, cider royal, and mimbo (a mixture of rum and muscovado sugar). Imagine the small but thriving furnace and forge towns of the past—Washington, Mount, Quaker Bridge, and Martha. You may spot the vestiges of these settlements in a remnant of a foundation, in a cellar hole, or in some slag pebbles found on the ground.

This is also state forest country; the first one you'll drive through from Tuckerton is Bass River State Forest. You'll cross Wading River and Beaver Run in that area, followed by the deserted towns named above. Next come Wharton State Forest and the Batsto River. A total of 35 miles will take you to Berlin, called Long-a-Coming during its heyday.

If conditions prohibit driving Tuckerton Road, try one of the following paved routes through the barrens, or forget wheeled vehicles altogether and drag out your canoe, which is said to be the best way to see the barrens. These paved roads will have more traffic, of course, but they also take travelers to existing towns worth visiting.

Route 70 is a main highway running from east to west in the northern part of the pines. As such it will give you a view of the area in a hurry, guiding you through Lebanon State Forest and on to Philadelphia.

Route 206 runs north to south in the western portion of the barrens. On the way is the town of Tabernacle, a good example of today's pine towns. Route 563 also runs north to south, but it takes you right through the center of the barrens and to the town of Chatsworth. Chatsworth is the hub of the pines. There you'll find such quaint sites as Buzby's General Store, where local residents still socialize over coffee and conversation. Route 563 also takes you to Hog Wallow, a particularly interesting pine town.

Route 542 passes through the south portion of the pine forests and runs through Batsto, a partially restored iron-making village that's fun to see.

Lots of other side trips can be made from these roads. You might want to visit some of the other towns in the area. If you go to Waretown, near the shore, you can hear the fiddler who plays every Saturday night. Or start your trip on Long Beach and visit the famous Barnegat Light.

SOUTHEASTERN NEW JERSEY (The Cape)

Scenic drives

Ocean Drive: 40 miles through Atlantic and Cape May counties. From Atlantic City to Cape May Point—drive the "Flight of the Gulls" over a string of bridge-connected islands with ocean and inland bays, lighthouses and boardwalks, Victorian villages and charming resorts.

Constructed in 1940 to connect the resorts of Atlantic City and Cape May Point, Ocean Drive is aptly called "The Flight of the Gulls," guiding drivers over a string of islands connected by five bridges. The road runs through the 14 resort towns between Atlantic City and Cape May Point, offering views of the majestic Atlantic Ocean to the east and calm inland bays and meadows to the west. In many ways these Jersey shore resorts are typical of the East Coast ocean resorts that exist anywhere from North Carolina to New England. The atmosphere is made up of lighthouses, fishing piers, often-crowded beaches, the usual seaside tourist attractions and traps, and that delightfully refreshing salt air.

If you happen to have spent your childhood summers at some Atlantic shore resort, you will probably want to skip this trip. Many former Jersey shore vacationers maintain that the whole area has gone downhill. But whether it has or not, it continues to attract hordes of sun followers in the summer, making traffic heavy on the Ocean Drive during peak seasons. If you'd like to see the Jersey cape but can't take the traffic, try Route 9, which runs parallel with Ocean Drive, west of the Garden State Parkway (see *Scenic drives,* page 000).

If you don't mind a little traffic, there are other attractions that make Ocean Drive worthwhile. This area was the first Atlantic Coast resort area, and its modern resort facilities are intermixed with historic sites and peaceful back roads. If you've never been to Atlantic City, the next couple of years should prove an interesting time to see this famous resort town. With gambling now allowed, Atlantic City has taken on the appearance of a town going through its second childhood. Along with the casinos, other signs of the town's hope for new prosperity have sprouted all over. Rumor has it that there will be a Playboy hotel on the boardwalk and that Gucci and Neiman-Marcus are considering setting up shop there. The hope of most local residents is, of course, that today's tacky will turn into tomorrow's glamour and that everybody who lives in Atlantic City will get a piece of the action. But many of the resort's year-round residents are afraid that when prosperity returns to Atlantic City, no room will be left for them. With the tacky might go the flavor that keeps that city alive and different from younger resorts. And you might not be able to see boardwalk fortune tellers like Madame Susie or the hot-dog vendors who have spent a lifetime on that boardwalk. For the wheeler-dealers taking advantage of Atlantic City's prospects, nothing could be more fortuitous. But if Atlantic City loses its past and becomes another Las Vegas, it could also lose its charm. The next couple of years should tell which way the town will go.

Atlantic City is the starting point for this Ocean Drive tour. If you decide to skip it, enter Ocean Drive via Route 563 from Northfield. Remember that the road has a different name in each town. The length of time this tour will take is up to you: it can run anywhere from an hour or two to several days, depending on whether you stop to sightsee. While summer is the best season to see the shore in action, in spring and fall there are fewer crowds.

In Atlantic City, Ocean Drive becomes Atlantic Avenue. The first landmark on the trip is the Atlantic City Light near the Atlantic City Marina. From there, head south through Atlantic City, stopping where you wish. One interesting spot is the last of the famous Planter's Peanut shops, at 1011 Boardwalk. You might also note some of the street names on your route. You'll feel as if you're walking along a living Monopoly board.

South of Atlantic City, you'll pass the seaside towns of Ventnor, Margate, and Longport on the way to Ocean City. To reach Ocean City, you'll cross the first of the bridges, Longport Bridge. The toll for each bridge is 25 cents. You can buy a book of five tickets for $1 at any of the toll booths.

Almost as popular as Atlantic City, Ocean City is at the northern border of Cape May County, stretched out over eight miles of ocean beach. Ocean Drive is Wesley Avenue in the north section of town and Central Avenue in the south. Off the boardwalk at Moorlyn Place (near 8th Street) you'll find Music Pier, where nightly concerts are held during summer. If your timing is good, you can see the nation's oldest and largest baby parade.

At Strathmere, cross Corson Inlet Bridge and then drive by Whale Beach to Sea Isle City, another popular resort. Ocean Drive becomes Landis Avenue here. The attractions are five miles of beach, good seafood restaurants, and Ludlam Beach Light on the ocean.

Next is Townsend's Inlet Bridge, connecting Townsend's Inlet and Avalon. Follow Third Avenue in Avalon to stay on Ocean Drive, and watch visitors and residents alike surf fishing, crabbing, and admiring the local waterfowl.

Stone Harbor is the next town you'll come to; Ocean Drive continues to be Third Avenue. The main attraction here is Stone Harbor Bird Sanctuary. This heronry is a registered natural landmark, with a parking lot from which drivers can view the 21 acres of waterfowl territory.

Next, you drive over Nummy Island to Grassy Sound Bridge. That bridge leads to the Wildwoods, a string of three beautiful seaside towns. In North Wildwood, Ocean Drive is New Jersey Avenue. Just as you enter the town, you'll pass Hereford Inlet Light. Originally called Anglesee, this town provided the outlet to offshore fishing through Hereford Inlet. In Wildwood and Wildwood Crest, Ocean Drive is Atlantic Avenue. The three towns boast a five-mile beach, and Wildwood has a three-mile boardwalk.

Past Diamond Beach, you'll cross the Middle Thorofare Bridge. Ocean Drive takes you around the west side of Cape May Harbor, to Cape May City. The drive runs in a sort of circle around the city, following Pittsburgh Avenue to Beach Avenue, to Sunset Boulevard. Cape May is a fascinating city, as well as a veteran resort visited by several U.S. presidents. The flavor is Victorian. A trip through the village roads shows you a charming world (see *Country roads,* page). Among the sites are a horse-drawn trolley, a restored Victorian village, a museum, a boardwalk, and beaches that are covered with the famous Cape May diamonds—pebbles of almost pure quartz that glint like diamonds in the sun. Cape May is truly the nation's oldest resort, first explored in 1621 by Cornelius Jacobsen Mey, a representative of the Dutch West India Company.

From Cape May, drive to the tiny town of Cape May Point. The beaches on the Delaware Bay are covered with the Cape May diamonds, and you'll drive by Cape May Light. Also around Cape May Point are Witmer Stone Wildlife Sanctuary and Lake Lily, with its sand dunes, holly, marshes, and water-fowl. You can also see the remains of two shipwrecks at Cape May Point: the HMS *Martin* and the weird concrete ship, *Atlantis.*

This is where the Ocean Drive ends, but you can extend your oceanside tour by taking the ferry to Lewes, Delaware. At the end of the Garden State Parkway, drive west to Lincoln Boulevard, where you will find the ferry terminal just south of North Cape May.

The ferry from Cape May runs from around 7:30 A.M. until 6:30 P.M., with only about four scheduled departures year-round. Extra ferries run during the summer, but the schedule does change, so be sure to check your timing. Otherwise you might have to drive all the way around the bay. From Lewes the tour continues to Ocean City, Maryland (see *Scenic drives, Delaware*).

Shore Road (U.S. route 9): 30 miles through Cape May County. From Ocean City to Cape May City—nineteenth-century churches and historic homes, parks, and a fascinating hedge garden.

Although U.S. Route 9 is called Shore Road in Cape May County, it is not actually on the beach and serves as an inland alternative to the Ocean Drive. Route 9 runs west of and parallel to Ocean Drive and the Garden State Parkway, and usually has less traffic than those two routes during the area's peak season. Route 9 also offers a look at our colonial heritage, as you drive through villages and towns founded during America's early years. Where Ocean Drive offers sparkling ocean beaches and lively resorts, Route 9 has rural countryside and peaceful country roads.

Begin your drive at the 16th Street surf in Ocean City. Poking out of the ocean froth you'll see the rudder control of the four-masted *Sindia,* which ran aground there in December, 1901. Drive north to 9th Street and go west to Route 52. Take Route 52 west to Somers Point; just west of that town, take Route 9 south.

From Somers Point to Cape May, you'll find numerous country road stops to lure you out of your car. In the area between the intersection with Route 50 at Seaville and the intersection with Route 28 near South Seaville, there are several sights worth seeing. In the town of Seaville, don't miss the Seaville Friends Meeting. The 1716 church is constructed principally of the cedar that grows in the area. Moved to Seaville from the town of Beesley's Point in 1731, the building has an exterior siding that was added in 1883.

Another church you'll pass is the Seaville Methodist. The existing church was built in 1857, but the graveyard is much older. Gravestones of well-known area families, such as the Townsends, go back as far as 1788.

If you're interested in old churches like these, you can jog right (west) onto Route 28 toward South Seaville. On South Dennis Road you'll find the Seaville Camp Meeting. Built in 1864, the church is surrounded by charming little cottages with lacy ornamentation that's worth noting.

Return to Route 9 to Ocean View. On the corner of South Seaville Road and Route 9 is Calvary Baptist Church. Erected on land donated by Joshua Townsend in 1811, the church was built between 1853 and 1855, with the modern educational wing added in 1955.

Proceed south on Route 9 to Clermont. Watch for the house of Mr. and Mrs. John Enright. Recently restored by the owners, the 1776 house has cedar floors and planked walls. The beautiful grounds are covered with large maple, spruce, and cedar trees.

Just before you reach the county seat, Cape May Court House, you'll drive by Cape May County Park. This is a pretty place to stop for a picnic or just commune with the 50 species of birds, 30 species of wildlife, and more than 24 types of trees.

The town of Cape May Court House is also worth a few stops. On Route 9, you'll pass the Cape May County Historical Museum, housed in an old home. Once in Cape May Court House, head for Main Street. An interesting site is the old county courthouse. Built in 1848, the building has a notable bell tower and a finely detailed exterior. Note the cornice and window trim. In 1927 a new courthouse was built.

Also on Main Street is the Jonathan Hand Office, now used by the Red Cross. The structure, built aroud 1801, was named for its original owner, a Cape May County clerk who was captain of the Cape May Militia during the War of 1812.

South of the county seat, there are sightseeing opportunities galore, many of them taking drivers off Route 9 on short side trips through the southwestern portion of the county. From Cape May Court House, drive about 10 miles, past the town of Erma, to Tabernacle Road. Turn right (west) on Tabernacle Road and drive past Shunpike Road. Near the county airport you'll find Bennett's Bog Wildlife Sanctuary, which is full of flora and fauna not usually found in the area.

Another outdoor attraction—made by man rather than nature—is the Hedge Gardens in the town of Fishing Creek. One mile from Wildwood Villas and six miles from Wildwood, the gardens can be reached by following the signs directing drivers to the county airport. At the airport entrance blinker, go south on Breakwater Road. There you'll find the gardens—the result of 40 years of fascinating work. Beginning the work as a hobby, Gus Yearicks sculpted hedge pieces on his property into nearly every shape you can think of. This creative gardener has put in more than 35,000 hours creating such items as a whole baseball game, Santa Claus with his reindeer, and dozens of animals. A hedge carved in the shape of the ocean liner *Queen Mary* took Yearicks 18 years to complete. These hedges will enthrall your family and should not be missed while you are in this area. Donations are accepted at the Hedge Gardens; Yearicks' fascinating creations are well worth a contribution.

The following are three other side trips you can take, depending on time. The Eli Teal House in the town of Fishing Creek is an odd building that looks like two houses fastened together. Built in 1827, this house is constructed of hand-hewn, wooden-pegged white oak. From Fishing Creek you can drive to the Villas to see the doll and toy collection and exhibit of Mr. and Mrs. John R. Scholtz. The collection, at 201 W. Drumbed Road, includes old iron toys, walking dolls, and other fascinating toys. Be sure to ask to see the doll furniture made by Mr. Scholtz from a 100-year-old pattern. The third side trip takes you to the town of Cold Spring. The Jonathan Hoffman property is located at the intersection of Jonathan Hoffman and Bayshore roads. The huge main house, build in 1870, is now closed. The owner, Mrs. Robert Ridpath, now lives in "Graylone," a studio home and garden on the property. After you've chosen your side trips, you can return to Route 9 and proceed to Cape May City and Cape May Point. You'll find lots of attractions there to end your Route 9 tour (see *Ocean Drive,* page 73, for details).

Upper Cape May Circle tour: 38 miles through north-central Cape May County. From Seaville to Belleplain and back—an autumn drive through Great Cedar Swamp and Belleplain State Forest.

Mention the Jersey cape and most of us think of seashore. This circle tour, on the other hand, shows travelers the inland side of Cape May County. Winding around a series of connected country roads, it is a scenic route that's at its best during the fall. Deciduous hardwood trees, combined with the local pines, laurel, and holly, form a profusion of color during the autumn months.

The circle itself is centered around Woodbine, the region's industrial hub, but the following route does offer a country atmosphere. If you're especially energetic, you can do this tour by bicycle.

Start the drive or bike ride in Seaville, at the junction of

Routes 9 and 50. Drive south on Route 9 (Shore Road) past Magnolia Lake. Turn right (west) on South Dennis-Ocean View Road, and drive about three miles to South Dennis. From there take Route 47 about two miles to North Dennis-Marshallville Road (Route 557). Turn right (north) onto Route 557 and drive about one-half mile. Then turn left onto East Creek Mill Road, and drive about two miles to Belleplain Road. This area is Belleplain State Forest, one of the prettier sections of the drive. Turn right (north) onto Belleplain Road and drive three or four miles to Route 49. Take Route 49 east about two or three miles to Tuckahoe. Then take Route 50 south to Petersburg two to three miles. Around Petersburg you should come upon the Great Cedar Swamp area. From there, turn left onto Tuckahoe Road and drive one mile to Tyler Road. Turn right (south) onto Tyler Road and drive another mile to Greenfield Road. Take Greenfield Road south to Route 50, a little more than a mile. Route 50 will take you back to Seaville, about two miles.

Country roads

Victoriana-plus: three miles through Cape May City. From museums to mansions—gimcracks, gewgaws, and gingerbread; historic houses and hotels in America's first resort.

Cape May City holds several claims to fame. Besides being an attractive vacation area, the city is a real mecca for history buffs. Those who admire Victoriana, in fact, could hardly find a site that offers more examples of the charms of Victorian America. Keep in mind that this city is still popular with summer vacationers and consider touring it during fall, winter, or spring. The attractions are mostly manmade, so the season is really irrelevant. If the weather is nice, you can do the tour by bicycle or on foot rather than by car.

Enter Cape May City from the north, via Route 9 or the Ocean Drive. Starting at Washington Street, which runs parallel to Lafayette Street, drive to the corner of Washington and Schellenger streets. The Emlen Physick Estate, at 1050 Washington Street, is the home of the Mid-Atlantic Center for the

Arts and the Cape May County Art League. Built in 1881, the estate includes a museum and offers guided tours of the house. Continue south on Washington to Jefferson Street. At 720 Washington Street, you'll find a good example of a Victorian house, complete with ornate brackets and a cupola.

Turn left at the next block, Franklin Street, and right onto Hughes Street. Keep an eye out for 655 Hughes Street. The house has finely detailed window trim. It is said to be one of the best examples of Victorian restoration in town. At 609 Hughes Street, you'll find one of the older houses on the tour. The Hughes House was built in 1838 in the colonial style.

Cross Ocean Street, and turn right onto Decatur Street. Make a left onto Carpenters Lane and another left onto Jackson Street. Note the Gibson House at 45 Jackson Street. The typically Victorian detail on this house can be seen on the roof shingles and cornices. Drive down Jackson Street to Beach Avenue (also Ocean Drive), turn right, and turn right again onto Perry Street.

Facing Atlantic Terrace is an interesting group of houses built for seven sisters around 1880. You'll also pass the Pink House, built around 1879. It's hard to miss this one, since it is one of the most ornate houses in the town.

From Perry Street turn left onto Congress Place. Numbers 205 and 207 are beautiful houses, noted for their verandas overlooking the ocean and, above, their cast-iron widow's walks—vestiges of the town's earlier fishing days. On the other side of the street is Congress Hall. This structure served as a vacation retreat for six former U.S. presidents. It was built in 1879.

Turn right onto Congress Street, left onto South Lafayette Street, and left onto Windsor Street. There you'll find the Windsor Hotel, built in 1878. The hotel, a good example of late Victorian style architecture, is named for the queen they called the Widow of Windsor.

Turn left onto Beach Avenue (Ocean Drive) and drive north along the shore to Jefferson Street, where you turn left. From here the tour twists and backtracks through the city. You can choose how much of it you wish to drive. Turn left onto

Stockton Avenue, pass Franklin Street, and turn right onto
Howard Street. On the block between Sewell and Columbia
avenues, you'll find historic Chalfonte Hotel. The hotel escaped
the 1878 fire that destroyed much of the city, leaving the
Chalfonte as Cape May's oldest large hotel. It was erected in
1876 by Civil War hero Henry Sawyer and has seen a lot of
action. Don't be surprised if you feel the spirits of Cape May's
nineteenth-century citizens wandering through the corridors.

At this point, turn left onto Columbia Avenue and then left
again onto Gurney Street. At 635 Columbia Avenue is an 1856
Victorian mansion, built as a club for Southern gentlemen. The
building was designed to look like an Italian villa, and if you go
inside, you'll see some of the original furniture. The Bolt House,
at 26 Gurney Street, is all original, built in 1869. Also on this
block is the Colonial Hotel. Actually built during the late
Victorian period, the white clapboard building is noted for its
turrets and whimsical fish-scale shingles. Perhaps ahead of its
time, the hotel was built to include gas lights, steam heat, and
electric bell systems.

From this point on, the rest of the tour is up to you. You can
leave the city via Ocean Drive north or continue driving through
these quaint streets. To make a complete circle, return to
Jefferson Street (west) and turn right (north) when you reach
Washington Street.

SOUTHWESTERN NEW JERSEY (Delaware Bay)

Scenic drives

Route 49 and the Delaware Bay: about 50 miles through Salem
and Cumberland counties.

Southwestern New Jersey probably is the least interesting area in
the state. The terrain is mainly flat, and the proximity of
Philadelphia and its metropolitan area contributes to the lack of
natural beauty. Your best bet when driving this area is to take
Route 49 south from the Delaware Memorial Bridge, bearing
south off the highway to follow the coastline. The territory
farther inland really is not worth seeing.

Near Pennsville, a few miles south of the bridge, are several sightseeing opportunities. At the Kelly's Point-Finn's Point area, you can stop and visit Finn's Point National Cemetery, Fort Mott, and the Killcohook National Wildlife Refuge. Basic park facilities are offered, but there's no camping.

Continuing on Route 49, cross Salem Cove to the town of Salem. This is a good point at which to cut south toward the bay on any of the surrounding country roads. Watch for signs directing you to Hancock's Bridge, where you can visit the Hancock House and Greenwich Monument near Springtown and Cohansey.

If you decide to continue on Route 49 rather than jogging off onto country roads, head for Gouldtown. From there you can get onto Route 553 south. This is a fairly scenic route, winding through land dotted and coursed with creeks and lakes. A good stopping point on Route 553 is Port Norris.

Country roads

As is the case with scenic routes, there are no great country roads in this part of New Jersey. If you want to try hunting for them anyway, stick to the towns along the Delaware River and Delaware Bay.

4

New York

Cross-state drives

Route 9: about 340 miles through Westchester, Putnam, Dutchess, Columbia, Rensselaer, Saratoga, Warren, Essex, and Clinton counties. From the Big Apple to the world's largest McIntosh orchard—following the colonial water route, up the Hudson River, and along the banks of Lakes George and Champlain.

For the most part, New York's Hudson Valley has an unexpectedly pristine beauty all of its own, except, of course, near its New York City estuary. Alas, the Big Apple itself has suffered many bruises over the years, and many of the natural wonders that awed Henry Hudson more than 300 years ago today are obscured by the New York megalopolis. For those of you who dislike cities, traveling Route 9 north as a scenic route to Canada should be a rewarding trip. Although the valley land is pretty much the same all the way along the state's eastern border, the green mountains, rushing waters, and dense forests that characterize the state intensify as you proceed north. By the time you've reached the lovely village of Garrison (about 60 miles north of Gotham) you'll forget you ever hated the Hudson.

At Garrison, the primeval Hudson seems to reappear. There's little sign of the pollution that has plagued the eyes and noses of New Yorkers for decades. The river narrows and begins to curve, with graceful willows swaying on its green banks.

For those who are willing to venture into the jungle of New York City, there are details on little-known paths there in Chapter 6. To avoid the city entirely, begin the trip in northern Westchester County, where rural New York begins. Wherever you plan to start, you can stop at many irresistible vacation sites that have something for every season. And if you're just making your way toward Canada, try taking Route 9 all the way as an alternate route to Interstate 87, the New York State Thruway in southern New York and the Adirondack Northway in the north. While Interstate 87, too, is scenic, it provides limited access to the smaller and often more historic towns in the valley, and its major highway speed requirements give you little time to linger, even visually.

Starting in New York City, or anywhere in lower Westchester County, Route 9 is Broadway, once known as the Albany Post Road. Following the course of the Hudson, this road probably has been traveled more often than almost any other in the country. The Hudson could be called the oldest continuously significant river in the history of the United States. Its waters and banks were known to early seventeenth-century explorers, to hardy Indians that lived in these mountain woods, to the soldiers of the Revolutionary War, and to generations of citizens, from the pioneers to the residents of today's cities. Even in its real wilderness sections, you might see a canoer wending his way down the Hudson, and where there isn't a city, there's a charming community dating back to pioneer America.

If you prefer to skip Broadway in New York, you can take the Henry Hudson Parkway (Route 9A) north to its intersection with Route 9 near Van Cortlandt Park in the Bronx, just south of the New York City-Yonkers line. In this stretch of the road about the only thing you'll see that Hudson also saw are the magnificent palisades on the river's west bank. Even these have been saved from industrialization only by local preservation efforts.

The south suburbs you'll drive through on Route 9 are principally old river towns, and as such, many of them are not completely gorgeous. There are still many old, and some historic, mansions built on the bluffs overlooking the river. Watch for these from the car, but avoid them if you don't like company. If you're up to touristy sightseeing, you can stop at Philipse Manor on Yonkers' Riverdale Avenue (parallel to Route) 9). Also in Yonkers is the Hudson River Museum, in Trevor Park off Warburton Avenue. In Dobbs Ferry there is the Livingston Manor House, and in Irvington you can visit Sunnyside, the home of Washington Irving. In Tarrytown, you can stop at Lyndhurst, just south of the Tappan Zee Bridge. And in North Tarrytown you can see Sleepy Hollow Dutch Reformed Church in Kingsland Point Park. Another mansion, Philipsburg Manor, is to the east. Continue north on Route 9 (still Broadway) to Peekskill, about 40 miles north of Manhattan. In between you'll pass Sing Sing Prison of 1940s gangster movie fame—where the term "up the river" came from. Now, euphemistically—and officially—called the Ossining Correctional Facility for Men, the prison is in another old river town. There are some beautiful old and new houses in the residential areas overlooking the Hudson in the Briarcliff-Scarborough area.

The first really exurban stop along the way also is one of the most charming along the whole 300-mile route. About eight miles north of Peekskill is Garrison, a tiny Putnam County village of 1,600 people. Just a few miles south of Garrison, be sure to notice Manitoga, a nature preserve with some great walking trails. Just north of Manitoga is Dick's Castle, a real contractor's nightmare and a weird sight. Construction of it began in 1902. Workmen had spent nine years building the shell of this summer home, which is designed to look like the Spanish Alhambra, when the owner lost his money in the stock market and ordered the work stopped. Today you can see the eerie shell of this castle, but rumor has it that an Austrian engineer has bought it and plans to finish the work the hapless Dick began. For a great meal, drive a couple of miles north to the Bird and Bottle Inn, a high quality restaurant that offers tranquil meals in a colonial house.

To reach Garrison, take Route 403 west from Route 9, straight into the town at the intersection of Route 9D. At Garrison's Landing you'll find the shops and buildings that were used in the filming of the movie *Hello Dolly*. This town is really suited to that era, with a modest village green on the river and a tiny gazebo for the local band. There's an annual arts and crafts fair here during August. At any time of year, you'll feel as if you have stepped into another world when you enter Garrison, and there is a picturesque view across the river. The Hudson is relatively clean here, and you can see West Point, the U.S. Military Academy, across the river.

Drive about four miles north on Route 9D to Boscobel, another monster mansion of the type that nineteenth-century industrial barons loved to build here. The name *Boscobel* is taken from the Italian words meaning "beautiful woods." Boscobel is 175 years old. Beautifully restored, the former Dyckman Estate can be visited anytime except during January and February. Another imposing structure you'll pass when you return to Route 9 is the historic monastery of Atonement Friars, Greymoor. It is open to the public between June and October.

A couple of miles north, on Route 9D, is Cold Spring. At the foot of Main Street is The Station, a restaurant full of old photos and railroad memorabilia. From Cold Spring, you can take Route 9D back to Route 9 by driving east on Route 301. In the 25 miles between Cold Spring and Poughkeepsie, you'll drive through woods and modest hills, passing through Clarence Fahnestock Memorial Park, which has one ski slope. The towns are old river settlements, and residents as far north as Fishkill have been known to commute to New York City to make their livelihood. Along the way, you can stop at the Van Wyck Homestead or the First Dutch Reformed Church of Fishkill.

At Poughkeepsie you enter an urban-industrial area, with some well-frequented tourist sights to the north. Again, if you don't mind crowds, you can visit the Franklin Delano Roosevelt Home, the Vanderbilt Mansion, or the Mills Mansion—all off Route 9.

Between Poughkeepsie and Albany, you're in for a moderately pretty 65-mile drive. You can see the Catskills on the west side of the river and small valley towns in your path. In the town of Hudson is the American Museum of Fire Fighting (on Harry Howard Avenue), said to be one of the best of its kind in the country.

From Albany, the state capital, drive about 30 miles north to Saratoga Springs (see *Scenic drives, Eastern New York*). Drive another 17 miles to Glen Falls (see *Scenic drives, Eastern New York*).

Drive nine miles north to Lake George. There you reach a fork in Route 9 and Route 9N. If you take Route 9, you'll pass more wilderness territory, with points of interest and great scenery in the awesome Adirondack Mountains. These are the highest mountains in the Mid-Atlantic states, with Mount Marcy (about 10 miles west of Route 9) towering over the surrounding peaks at 5,344 feet. There are many other peaks of note. The small town of Chestertown along the way is famous as the burial place of John Butler Yeats, painter, writer, and father of William Butler Yeats. You'll also get a possibly crowded look at the Adirondack Natural Stone Bridge and Caves near Pottersville.

If you take Route 9N northeast from Lake George, you'll pass a large resort area that includes the vacation-oriented towns of Lake George Village, Diamond Point, Bolton Landing, and Hague. In Lake George Village you can feast your eyes on some of the nineteenth-century mansions that gave part of the town the nickname "Millionaires' Row." From Lake George, you can drive the fantastic Mount Prospect Parkway (see *Country roads, Northern New York*).

Diamond Point, three miles north of Lake George, is named for the stunning crystal rocks in the area. Drive seven miles north to the Lake George Narrows at Bolton Landing. Here the lake is rather a maze of barely navigable water courses wedged in between clusters of inlands.

North of Bolton Landing the road leaves the lake shore to amble over the Tongue Mountain range. A roadside overlook welcomes you back to the lake at Sabbath Day Point. Drive a few miles north to Silver Bay and Hague, resort towns set on a narrow strip of land, with sandy beaches and an over-the-shoulder view of Hague Mountain. At nearby Cook's Bay, you'll find the curious Indian kettle-holes in the shore rocks in which early Indians cooked their meals.

Drive to the tip of Lake George at historic Ticonderoga and take Route 9N around the eastern banks of Lake Champlain. Drive about nine miles west on Route 9N from Elizabethtown and go north at the intersection of Route 9, 23 miles to Keeseville. Continuing north, you will pass historic Lake Champlain, recreational parks, and such lovely spots as Ausable Point, Port Kent, and Valcour Island. From Ausable Chasm to Plattsburgh, you'll drive a total of about 16 miles. For details on the Plattsburgh area, see *Country roads, Northern New York.*

End your trip at the town of Champlain, in the middle of apple country, near the world's largest McIntosh orchard.

EASTERN NEW YORK (The Hudson and its Headwaters)

Scenic drives

Taconic Parkway: about 60 miles through Putnam, Dutchess, and Columbia counties. From Mahopac Falls to Lake Taghkanic—a wooded tour through Indian country.

Town names, street names, mountain ranges, even the name of the local swimming hole—almost everything in this region comes from an Indian language. Indian relics are almost as abundant in local museums as are Revolutionary War memorabilia.

This famous parkway, the longest one in New York, takes you through less spectacular land than the north offers, but it is close to New York City and much of it is relatively unspoiled. In some places you can almost hear the footsteps of our forefathers as they tramped along the river trails. The Taconic is a second choice if you're looking for speed and modern efficiency in roads. Like most of the old parkways emanating from New York, it was constructed for the pleasure cars of the 1920s and retains many of its original killer curves and narrow lanes. It has an old railing-type of divider through much of it, making it even more difficult to see in rainy weather, and is to be avoided in snow. Get on the parkway in lower Putnam County or somewhere in northern Westchester County. Avoid driving this route during rush hours, as it is a popular commuter route for suburbanites. The nicest thing about this southern stretch of the parkway is that it avoids the center of various towns. You'll pass hilly forest, streams, small ski areas, and state parks, such as Clarence Fahnestock Memorial Park, which has a ski slope. Another ski slope can be found by taking Route 84 west to the river town of Beacon. The Beacon area is really untamed, and if you're driving at night, your way will be dimly lit. The only sign of civilization is an occasional airplane blinker on a mountain-top.

From the Beacon area, you can drive about 45 miles north all the way to the Lake Taghkanic park area. If you yearn for civilization, you can turn west off the road from any point to see some of the old river towns. They're not usually pretty but they are interesting, many of them isolated on the shoreline.

West-bank parks tour: about 40 miles through Westchester and Orange counties. From Anthony's Nose to Seven Lakes— beautiful mountain tours, with a choice of pristine parks and a side-trip to historic West Point.

This short tour exemplifies the diversity of scenery and sightseeing attractions available within a short hop of New York City. Those who deride the Big Apple often are surprised at the natural wonders and get-away-from-it-all atmosphere to be found just north. This ride takes in popular as well as isolated spots.

Start the tour on Route 202, driving west from Yorktown Heights. Drive about 10 miles and pass Peekskill. You'll reach a traffic circle, where you drive straight on Bear Mountain Road toward the U.S. Army's Camp Smith. With the camp sign on your right and the Hudson on your left, begin your ascent of Anthony's Nose, the riverside peak named for the prominent proboscis of Mad Anthony Wayne of local Revolutionary War fame. This winding road takes you several miles up and around the peak, with a couple of scenic overlooks along the way for camera-wielders and the like. You'll pass several very old historic structures and arrive at the entrance to the Bear Mountain toll bridge.

Cross the bridge and take your choice of west-bank tours. You can go north on Storm King Highway (Route 9W). This is a less scenic route, but it leads to the U.S. Military Academy at West Point, which is worth a side trip if you have never seen it. You can take one of three exits off Route 9W—Highland Falls, Stony Lonesome, or Washington Gate. The academy campus is pretty and offers several overlooks of the river. Whatever you do, avoid West Point and the Storm King Highway on Saturdays during football season, unless you have access to a West Point schedule. The home games attract hordes of area fans to the stadium during the fall, making traffic unbearable.

If you bear southwest off the circle on Palisades Parkway, you can turn off on Seven Lakes Drive, near Harriman. This is a lovely seven- or eight-mile drive by the lake-dotted park area.

Routes 29 and 4: about 40 miles through Saratoga, Washington, and Warren counties. From Bemis Heights to Glens Falls— a huge Revolutionary War battlefield area around the Hudson River headwaters.

Saratoga, Washington, and Warren are lovely rural counties in the middle of the vast area called upstate New York. To residents of New York City, "upstate" means anything north of the Bronx, but to history buffs and vacationers alike, it often means the Saratoga Springs area.

To the wealthy set of the nineteenth century, Saratoga Springs' races and spas were a vacation haven that rivaled Newport, Rhode Island. About the same time that Atlantic City was in its heyday, in fact, Saratoga Springs was wowing the nouveau riche of the north country. Unfortunately, Saratoga Springs as a resort has suffered the same deterioration as did Atlantic City, and only once a year—in August, when the ponies are running—does the town reclaim its Gay Nineties glamour.

At any time of year Saratoga is still of historic interest. There are battlefields of the Revolutionary War in almost every direction from the town. The spas still draw health-seekers, although a recent investigation of the mineral waters found them high in radium. Because of this discovery, the state park now recommends mineral baths over mineral water drinks. But the Saratoga area residents—many of whom have been drinking the stuff all their lives—still swear by it. And they look pretty healthy.

Start your tour of this fascinating area at the Saratoga National Historical Park, at the intersection of Routes 4 and 32 just north of Bemis Heights. Drive west on Route 32 to the Visitor Center, where you may begin a nine-mile, self-guiding auto tour of the battlefield. If you follow Burgoyne's tide-turning southbound campaign from Montreal, the tour can take up to four hours.

Route 4 runs along the Hudson River. and from the battlefield you can drive about eight miles north to Schuylerville (the original town named Saratoga). There you'll find the country home of General Philip Schuyler, built around his farm and mill operation just after Burgoyne's 1777 surrender. In town, you'll find the Saratoga Battlefield Monument State Historical Site. At 21 Green Street you can drive to the top of the granite monument, passing bronze plaques that tell the story of the area battles.

From Schuylerville, drive west on Route 29 about 11 miles to Saratoga Springs. A mile south of the town, between Routes 9 and 50, is the Saratoga Spa State Park. In town are the Saratoga Historical Museum and the Walworth Memorial Museum.

Rexleigh, one of three covered bridges spanning Battenkill in Salem, New York, was built in 1874. *(Photo courtesy of Washington County)*

Historic Champlain
Barge Canal is banked
by pretty hillside
houses nestled among
the trees.
*(Photo courtesy of
Washington County)*

An interesting side trip takes you three miles west on Route 29 to the Petrified Gardens, a National Natural Landmark where you can see the remains of a huge reef that lay under a sea covering the area 300 million years ago. Backtrack on Route 29 to Route 4 (11 miles), and drive about 12 miles to Hudson Falls. In between, you'll drive west of Battenkill, a stream just north of Route 29, crossed by three of the four Washington County covered bridges. To follow the river path, take Route 70 east.

Drive about one mile north of the kill to Old Champlain Canal Lock 12, where you can picnic. About nine miles north, you'll pass Fort Edward, and in Hudson Falls, you'll find several historic sites.

From Hudson Falls, take Route 4 northwest to follow the route of Burgoyne's 1777 invading army. Or take Route 32B from Hudson Falls to Glens Falls, at the headwaters. This charming town has a wealth of cross-country ski trails, an historical association museum, and a library that has resources for investigating the history of the area.

Glens Falls is the gateway to Lakes George and Champlain (see *Route 9, Cross-state drives,* and *Northern New York, Country roads*). When it was nothing more than a tavern stop on the old military road, Glens Falls saw the likes of Ben Franklin, James Madison, and Thomas Jefferson, who stopped there. Jefferson called Lake George the most beautiful lake he'd ever seen.

For an interesting trip to wind up the tour, drive half a mile north of Glens Falls on Route 9 to the crossing of Butler Brook. There you'll find the "Half Way Post," a watering spot and the site of an old Picket Fort, used during the French and Indian and Revolutionary wars.

Country roads

Routes 35, 118 and 129: about 20 miles through Westchester County.

Westchester County, like much of the area north of Gotham, is full of rich woods broken here and there by huge cool reservoirs that supply water to the city slickers. This short tour takes you through some of northern Westchester's in between-town areas and past several scenic dam sites.

Start on Route 35, traveling west toward Somers in Putnam County. You'll drive by occasional houses, hills, and woods.

You will come to a suddenly open hilly field on your left—the Lasdon Estate. Just past its well-mown "lawn," turn left on Wood Street at the sign to the Lasdon Bird Sanctuary. The sanctuary is nothing but land dedicated as wildlife refuge, so don't look for landmarks or a Visitor Center. The road gives you a chance to park on the side and get out for a walk along Amawalk Stream or through the woods (on the right side only). You'll drive through a sparsely populated residential area over several small bridges that cross the curving creek.

Backtrack on Wood Street, turning left on Route 35 at its end. Drive about one or two miles and look for Amawalk Dam. The road curves sharply near the dam. You can park in the small turn-around space to your right. The dam area is off

(Above) This path leads to the banks of Amawalk Stream in eastern New York. It is often used by local residents and fishermen out for a woodland stroll. (Below) Maximum speed allowed on highway curves like this one is about fifteen miles per hour. In the background are the dam and spillway on Amawalk Reservoir in eastern New York.

The rushing waters of the Croton Dam spillway can sometimes be heard by drivers going past on the nearby road, although the dam itself is not visible from the road.

limits, but you can walk into the woods on the left side of the street, wandering the trails along beautiful Amawalk Stream, a trout fisherman's paradise.

Continue west on Route 35 toward Yorktown Heights. At the traffic light in the town, which is not very scenic, go straight on Route 35-118. At the next traffic light, turn right on Underhill Road, traveling about three miles past a residential area that contains some interesting houses. At the end of the road, turn right on Route 129 at the edge of Croton Reservoir. Route 129 winds a couple of miles through the woods, leaving the reservoir shore and eventually taking you to Croton Dam (on the left). Take the steep driveway down to the park area, where you can picnic near the thundering waters of the spillway. From the park you can go another five miles or so to the town of Croton-on-Hudson, another old river town. Croton has some pretty residential neighborhoods in the hills overlooking the river, but it's not really worth a side trip. From the town you can head for Route 9 and parts north.

Colonial New York tour: a look at 10 miles of colonial roads in Yorktown Heights.

Yorktown Heights and surrounding villages are full of the "Washington Slept Here" genre of historic sites. Many Revolutionary War and pre-war structures still stand. Although it is surrounded by tiny, well-planned villages with townhouses and country estates, Yorktown was mainly a rural town until just about 20 years ago. Most of its historic buildings, rather than being in the middle of today's merchant-business district, were farmhouses or roadside taverns and are scattered through the 40-square-mile town. The following are a couple of the most interesting back roads in the area, offering the most authentic colonial flavor.

Start on Route 129, driving east from Croton. Cross the short span bridge that runs over the Croton Reservoir, and watch for the first left turn—Hunterbrook Road. The road winds through a woodsy area by the lake, so thick with trees that you can't see the lake at all during the summer. Old houses are tucked into

Yorktown's old Baptist Church is surrounded by tombstones marking the graves of early church members. Some tombstones date as far back as the early 1800s.

the wooded area, many with ponds or creeks crossing their lush property. After a few miles, begin looking for Baptist Church Road on your right. The road is marked by and named for the little clapboard church on the corner, Baptist Church, typical of these farm-and-woods churches of the colonial Hudson Valley, with gravestones dating back to the early 1800s.

Drive really slowly along the road, which has blind curves and barely enough room for two lanes of traffic. You'll pass stately old farmhouses and newer summer houses in Tudor and other styles. My favorite house in the area is off to the right, on a dip in the road. Almost completely hidden by trees during the summer, this beautifully placed redwood house is surrounded by a moat fed by a nearby stream.

At the end of Baptist Church Road, turn left on Baldwin Road. Baldwin Road crosses the Taconic Parkway and proceeds back to Yorktown, intersecting Route 202 just west of the center of town.

CENTRAL NEW YORK (Farm Country)

If you're looking for spectacular views, this section of New York is probably the least interesting of all. While most of it is rurally scenic, it seems to have just a little bit less of what the rest of the state has—fewer mountains, lower heights, less water, and fewer parks. The exception to the rule is the weather. The unfortunate residents of the Oneonta area are blessed with more rain than most of the state.

All is not lost here, of course. The terrain certainly isn't unpleasant; it's just difficult to single out one or two routes as specially scenic or otherwise noteworthy. Your best bet is to pick and choose at random if you happen to be in the area.

For starters, you can try driving Route 28 north, from Oneonta to Cooperstown. This 25-mile tour will lead you to the Cooperstown National Baseball Hall of Fame. Founded by James Fenimore Cooper's father, Cooperstown is rife with allusions and monuments to the pioneers of the *Deerslayer* era. The town has almost overdone it in the way of museums. Besides a Farmer's Museum, depicting New York frontier life between 1790 and 1860, you can visit the Fenimore House, the Carriage and Harness Museum and an Indian museum. North of Cooperstown, stop at Busch Woodlands and Museum, which features Clydesdale horses and dioramas of scenes from Cooper's *Deerslayer*.

An interesting out-of-town sight is the old Kingfisher Tower, a replica of a castle built on "Glimmerglass," the name Cooper gave Lake Otsego.

As for the rest of the central region, you are on your own. For scenic routes, just meander over the township roads, minor highways, and county roads, avoiding the urban areas of Rome, Utica, and Syracuse.

NORTHERN NEW YORK (The Adirondacks and the Seaway)

Scenic drives

St. Lawrence Scenic Highway (Route 12): about 25 miles through Jefferson and St. Lawrence counties. From Alexandria Bay to Morristown—a thousand islands with a thousand diversions.

It seems a little odd to include a trip to the Thousand Islands and the St. Lawrence River in a guide to the Mid-Atlantic States. The road does run through the "Mid-Atlantic" state of New York, but the feel is of Canada. The border between countries runs right up the middle of the St. Lawrence, and it's difficult enough to distinguish one island from another without trying to tell Canadian territory from American. To be slightly more accurate than the name, there are more than 1,700 deep green islands in this chaotic 30-mile seaway stretch. The St. Lawrence is quite a sight, and if you associate the term *Mid-Atlantic* only with the sand-and-seagull air of Maryland, you'll find this territory refreshingly different.

Everything is water-oriented here. You're likely to spot every kind of craft you can imagine, from sightseeing boats and fishing craft to cumbersome ocean steamers. A lot of this land is still frontier land, and Indian lore abounds. If you start at the

Alexandria toll bridge, you can explore the river islands. The St. Lawrence Scenic Highway (Route 12) begins a few miles north at Alexandria Bay, known to the locals as Alex Bay. Route 12 runs north along the river banks to Morristown. All along the way you'll see anglers fishing for muskie, walleye, bass, and pike. From Alexandria Bay, you might be able to see Boldt Castle on one of the islands—a millionaire's crumbling old hideaway.

If you go north on Route 12, you'll be able to get out to stretch your legs at one of several river overlooks. You'll drive by Keenaydin State Park (to your right) and Goose Bay. Farther north, on your left, will be Thousand Island Park, followed by the wily path of Crooked Creek. Drive north to Chippewa Bay and Cedar Island State Park.

The next large state park you'll pass is Jacques Cartier, with the huge Black Lake region off to your right. Drive a few miles north and end your trip at Morristown, near the intersection of Routes 12 and 37. If you can't stand to part ways with the river, continue along its banks on Route 37 to Massena about 45 glorious miles northeast.

Adirondack Trail (Route 30): about 160 miles through Franklin, Hamilton, Fulton, and Montgomery counties. From Malone to Amsterdam—crossing the wilderness of Adirondack Park's cabin country.

Saranac Lake, Long Lake, Indian Lake, and Cranberry Lake— these are but a few of the hundreds of watering holes that draw modern wilderness seekers from all regions of New York to this nature garden. The land is hilly at least, mountainous at most, and the predominant structures are the wooden cabins and rustic lodges that are filled with vacationers during the summer and fall months. Even during the peak season, the loudest daytime sound you're likely to hear is the buzz of an outboard motor; at night the hum of the crickets takes over. Waterskiers weave their wakes across the recreational lakes such as Long Lake, while landlubbers hike the cool woods on the shores.

Many of the towns you'll pass bear the names of the lake that most strongly influences the land; sometimes a local mountain is so honored—towns called Indian Lake, Raquette Lake, and Blue Mountain Lake; peaks named Three Pond Mountain, Twin Lakes Mountain, and Spruce Lake Mountain. Start your tour in the north country of Franklin County, in the town of Malone. The elevation here is well under 1,000 feet, but if you drive 15 miles south on Route 30 you'll enter Adirondack Park. When you reach Lake Titus you'll see Debar Mountain in the distance—elevation 3,305. Through this sudden climb, you'll pass Meacham Lake and its campsite. About 17 miles from Lake Titus is the town of Paul Smiths. Pass popular Saranac Lake to the town of Tupper Lake, about 26 miles farther on. Another 26 miles south takes you to Long Lake, a rustic resort area. There are campsites all over this part of the park. Drive southwest about three miles to the town of Deerland and then eight miles to the town of Blue Mountain Lake. On the west side of the road, you can choose between Lake Eaton and Forked Lake campsites. Just north of the town of Blue Mountain Lake, stop and visit the Adirondack Museum. Just south of the town, you can use Lake Durant campsite.

Drive about 11 miles to Indian Lake, in the middle of the park. Here the mountains reach 3,400 feet into the invigorating air, and the tallest New York peaks can be seen towering in the northeast.

Travel the 26-mile lakeshore to Speculator, where Routes 8 and 30 join. Along the lakeshore you can detour to Lewey Lake campsite, Oak Mountain Ski Center, or Moffitt Beach. Drive 10 miles to the point where Route 8 forks off and then about 36 miles to Vail Mills. On this stretch of Route 30 you'll follow the Sacandaga River to the west bank of the Great Sacandaga Lake, passing Sacandaga campsite and Northampton Beach.

In the nine miles to Amsterdam you'll pass several historic sites. From Amsterdam, you can take a side trip west on Route 67 to Johnstown and Gloversville. In Johnstown you can visit Johnson Hall, the only baronial mansion ever built in America. The original building was erected in 1762 by Sir William Johnson, crown superintendent of Indian affairs and baronet during pre-Revolutionary War America.

Country roads

Prospect Mountain State Parkway: about six miles through Warren County.

This short toll road offers one of the best roadside views of Lake George and the Adirondacks. Winding to the top of Prospect Mountain, the road offers summit views 2,000 feet above the lake. The sails on Lake George look like little white and pastel-colored butterflies and from this height, the hordes of tourists below are all but nonexistent.

Start the tour on Route 9, a couple of miles south of Lake George Village. Drive north toward the tip of the lake and turn left onto the parkway, near Gaslight Village. As you wind slowly up the mountain, look for the three overlooks made available by the state. There is one at Rattlesnake Cobble, one at Big Hollow Branch, and one at the mountain's 2,021-foot summit. From the end-point parking lot, "viewmobiles" carry visitors to picnic areas at the top.

On a clear day you can look south toward Albany, east as far as New Hampshire's Mount Washington, and north, where you might see mile-high Mt. Marcy.

Warrensburg area arts and crafts jaunt: about 15 miles through Warren County.

Adirondack Park seems to attract almost as many artists and craftsmen as it does hunters, fishermen, and casual vacationers. Maybe it's the mountain air, or maybe it's the country silence, but people seem to create beautiful things with their hands up here. In almost any town in the Lake George area—and scattered elsewhere throughout the park—you'll find antique and craft shops. A group of these area craft workers have formed Adirondack Artisans, basing it in Glens Falls and dedicating it to the pursuit of crafts developed with native materials and under local influences. You'll find their exhibits in the libraries, galleries, schools, and museums of area towns. The following is a country-road type of crafts tour, where you're likely to discover many artisans hard at work in ceramics, quilting,

stained glass, blacksmithing, woodwork, weaving, and leatherworking.

Start in Warrensburg and leave the town by driving southwest
on River Street. The road runs along Schroon River and its
scenic rapids to the point where it joins the Hudson. You'll reach
Thurman Bridge about 10 miles from Warrensburg. Take the
main road west to the hamlet of Stony Creek, which is something of an artist's enclave. On Stony Creek Road you can visit
Gary Shumay's leatherworking shop. Deeper into the mountains
(west) is Harrisburg Road, and furnituremaker Peric Waxweiler.
If you like Early American pieces, you shouldn't miss this shop.
Other artisans in the area include leatherworkers, potters, slate
painters, and feather strokers—John Cody, Todd Kelsy, and
Elsie Soto among them. Ask anyone in town where to find
them.

Plattsburgh area circle tour: 50 miles through Clinton County.

In a state which has a unique shape and irregular borders,
Clinton County has the distinction of serving as New York's
northeast corner. More than half of it falls into Adirondack
Park, with elevations of nearly three thousand feet in the
southwest portion. Clinton County is a land of apples and pines,
where deciduous hardwoods complement stately evergreens in a
splendor of autumn color. U.S. Route 9 through Plattsburgh
forms part of a scenic route from New York City to Montreal
(see *Cross-state drives, New York*), and if you make the trip
during the summer you'll find the pervasive quality of this
atmosphere to be green and fresh.

While not an aesthetic miracle in city planning, Plattsburgh is
far from an eyesore; it offers several interesting historic sites to
the driver. You'll find such frontier monuments as the Champlain Monument at Cumberland Avenue and the mouth of the
Saranac River, erected in memory of Champlain's discovery of
the lake in 1609. While you're there, visit the Kent-Delord
House Museum. It's right across the street from the monument.
British headquarters during the War of 1812, the building also is
noted as Plattsburgh's oldest house, built in 1797.

Explore the city as you will, leaving the urban area via Route
9 north. At the intersection with Interstate Route 87, turn right

(east) to Cumberland Head. On this peninsula, you'll pass Plattsburgh Beach, former fishing village of the Mohawk Indians, a state campsite, and many summer homes. Take special note of the ferry that takes passengers to South Hero, Vermont—it's been chugging across Lake Champlain for more than 150 years.

Four miles north of the Route 9-Route 87 intersection, turn right on Point au Roche Road, which will take you along the lake shore to Lake Shore Road. Turn right (north), and watch for a marker about five-and-a-half miles north that commemorates Jean LaFramboise. This history-making pioneer was driven from his homestead in 1777 by Burgoyne, only to return six years later and begin the first apple orchard in what was to become one of the great apple centers of the continent.

At the intersection of Lake Shore Road and Route 191, you'll find another first in American history. The Saxe house (not open to the public) was built of stone in 1822 and witnessed the construction of the first steamboat wharf between Whitehall, New York (about 100 miles south of Plattsburgh), and St. John's, Quebec (about 50 miles north of Plattsburgh).

Drive west on Route 191, about three miles to Chazy. Along the way, you'll pass an orchard that claims to be "the largest McIntosh orchard in the world," and the Alice T. Miner Colonial Collection and Museum, a restored stone house built in 1824 and now filled with early Americana. Between Chazy and Sciota, you can just enjoy the countryside or you can stop at one of several agricultural demonstration facilities. From Sciota, it's another three miles west to the mountain village of Altona, where you should bear left (south). Continue about a mile farther to the dam and powerhouse that provided the area's first electricity. Then bear right for three miles to the Crowley Corners stop sign, where you turn left. Take the first right, onto Rand Hill Road, and drive through eight' or nine miles of pastoral birch and maple forests, farms, and orchards. After you've gone a full nine miles you'll reach a scenic overlook spot, as well as a marker on the grounds of a private home noting an Adirondack survey made in 1872.

From here on in, it's downhill through cool and fragrant pine forests. At the crossroads, turn right onto Route 374, and then left (east) toward Plattsburgh. Outside the city you'll pass more orchards and farmland.

WESTERN NEW YORK (Finger Lakes)

Scenic drives

Iroquois Trail: about 200 miles through Steuben, Yates, Ontario, Seneca, Cayuga, Schuyler, and Tompkins counties. From Cayuga to Keuka—tracing the Finger Lakes, New York's cornucopia of crops.

Ever since the braves and squaws of the Iroquois Federation tribes called the Finger Lakes home, this unique spray of long, narrow lakes has inspired countless legends, scores of paintings, and books full of praise. The Indians thought the lakes were formed when God laid His hand on earth, forever blessing this land with unbelievable fertility. Other admirers have likened the lakes to the bear claws the Indians hung from their necklaces. On the drier side, scientists tell us the lakes were formed when glacial drift blocked the rushing flow of meltwaters and naturally impounded these phenomenal watering holes.

Whichever theory you choose, you'll be hard-pressed to put the Finger Lakes' beauty into mere words. The 11 lakes offer 600 miles of bountiful shoreline for recreational and commercial pursuits, and the mountains and hills veined with meandering streams form a perfect vacationland. It's almost an unlimited playground, perfect for long, exploratory drives. Some say the Finger Lakes region includes 9,000 square miles and 11 lakes—from Syracuse to Rochester and all the way from Lake Ontario to the Pennsylvania border. Purists are likely to insist that true Finger Lakes land lies only around the six largest lakes—Canandaigua, Keuka, Seneca, Cayuga, Owasco, and Skaneateles.

Wherever you drive in this vast region, you'll see the signs of a rich heritage: from the longhouses of the Iroquois Federation tribes, to the local participation in the Women's Suffrage Movement, to some of the first American dabblings in the occult, the Finger Lakes area is full of history.

Besides the ever-present lakes, the views are dominated by beautiful farms producing truckload upon truckload of potatoes, enough cabbages to call the area "sauerkraut capital of the world," and the grapes that go into New York's finest wines. If you draw an east-west line through the town of Penn Yan, on Keuka Lake's northern tip, you'll divide the area into its basic north and south sections. To the north, the villages and farms have a New England flavor that reflects the origins of the region's early settlers. In the south, the influence is Pennsylvanian. Almost every town is full of historic sites and delightful pre-Victorian houses, while the in-between areas offer almost 20 state parks and campsite areas.

The human element is of particular interest here. As is the case in several other Mid-Atlantic territories, the people of the Finger Lakes area usually can think of no other place they'd rather live. Finger Lakers have a deep respect for their bountiful land and a certain peace of mind that comes from attaining contentment from the earth and its offerings. A somewhat similar population can be found in New Jersey's Pine Barrens.

Some diverse Americans of note hailed from the Finger Lakes, including Susan B. Anthony, who was sentenced for illegally voting in the old town of Canandaigua. Stephen Douglas trained for the bar in that town, and in Seneca Falls Elizabeth Cady Stanton and Amelia Jenks Bloomer fought for women's rights. Ms. Bloomer, unfortunately, is better known for the baggy pants she wore, which most American women were doomed to wear for years of gym classes.

If you take a side trip to the little town of Hydesville, north of Newark, you'll find the former home of Margaret and Kate Fox. In the mid-1850s these sisters, who claimed to have all kinds of extrasensory powers, began a traveling seance show. A local octogenarian, John Drummond, feeling that he was called to the site, has constructed a replica of the Fox sisters' house. Fittingly, Mr. Drummond says he has been visited by heavenly apparitions at least twice.

If you visit the town of Palmyra during the summer, you may be there for the annual reenactment of Joseph Smith's discovery of the golden tablets of the Mormon faith.

Start the Finger Lakes tour in the city of Ithaca, at the southern tip of Cayuga Lake. Several of the gorges that characterize this land run right through town, and you can stop at various historic sites. From Ithaca, take Route 13 three miles northeast of the Cornell University campus to Sapsucker Woods. Part of the university holdings, this 180-acre tract is an interesting bird sanctuary, with a pond, trails, and an observatory.

Backtrack on Route 13 about five miles (two miles southwest of Ithaca) and visit Buttermilk Falls State Park. Buttermilk Creek rises 500 feet in one mile of rushing rapids and waterfalls. At the park's north end is an old mill with a waterwheel, built in 1847, which now houses a museum. Drive three miles southwest on Route 13 to Robert H. Treman State Park. Besides camping and swimming here, you can go wandering among the 12 waterfalls of Enfield Glen. This spectacular sight has served as the backdrop for many movies whose scripts called for the Old West or Alaska.

Return to Ithaca on Route 13 and turn north on Route 89. Running along the west bank of Cayuga Lake, the road takes you 45 scenic miles to the town of Seneca Falls. Along the way, you can stop at Taughannock Falls State Park (eight miles north of Ithaca). The main attraction here is a waterfall 215 feet high—that's 50 feet higher than Niagara Falls! The surrounding glen walls reach 400-foot heights. The Falls View Overlook in the park can be reached by car or foot trail. Three miles east of Seneca Falls is Cayuga Lake State Park, where beach activities are the main features. When you reach Route 20 past Bridgeport, turn northeast on that road and drive five miles to Montezuma National Wildlife Refuge. Here you can drive along the main pool and view migratory waterfowl during the spring and fall. Backtrack five miles on Route 20 to Seneca Falls, a historic town and a hot spot during the Indian days. The town is at the foot of Cayuga Lake, on the old Genesee Trail. Members of the Seneca, Cayuga, Onondaga, Oneida, and Mohawk tribes blazed the first trails here 400 years ago. From Seneca Falls, drive about three miles west on Route 20 to the town of Waterloo. Go another six or seven miles on Routes 20 and 5 to Geneva. One mile east of that town, at the junction of Routes 50, 20, and 96A, is Seneca Lake State Park. About four miles south of Geneva, on Route 96A, is the Rose Hill Mansion. Built in 1839, the Greek Revival house is open to the public between May and October. Drive about eight miles south on Route 96A to Sampson State Park, which lures visitors with its three miles of Seneca Lake waterfront.

Take Route 96A eight miles south to Ovid and drive south on Route 414, about 25 miles to Watkins Glen. There, you can stop at popular, but worthwhile, Watkins Glen State Park. Reached from the village and Route 414, the park has two miles of awesome gorge, where the stream drops 700 feet over waterfalls and rocks. There's a heart-thumping foot bridge that runs 165 feet above the gorge.

Take Route 14 south about three miles to Montour Falls. On Catherine Street (also Route 14) you'll find the Old Brick Tavern Museum. Also serving as a school and sanitarium over the last two centuries, the building is run by the Schuyler County Historical Society.

Backtrack to Watkins Glen and take Route 414 about 20 miles south to Corning. You can visit the Corning Glass Center there or walk through the Market Street restoration area. The restoration offers brick sidewalks, late eighteenth- and early nineteenth-century buildings, old shops, and a bona fide Gay Nineties' ice cream parlor, to say nothing of cheap, abundant public parking.

Take Route 17 northwest about 20 miles to the town of Bath, followed by Route 54 northeast about six miles to Hammondsport. This town is the hub of the Finger Lakes wineries, which you can tour (see *Country roads*).

Take Route 54A north along Keuka Lake, about 23 miles to Keuka Lake State Park. To reach this park, take Pepper Road off Route 54A to camping and other recreational facilities.

Seneca Trail: about 65 miles through Cattaraugus and Erie counties. From the Pennsylvania line to Hamburg—following an old Indian route through New York's southwest gateway.

The evidence—present and past—of American Indian culture is hard to miss in this territory, although it isn't the most scenic section of New York. Indian lore is the main attraction here. This western sample is included partly to offset the obvious omission of Niagara Falls, but it also makes a nice tour for Buffalo residents looking for a scenic break. Hamburg is about as close as you should get to Buffalo, which is not known for its sights. During winter, you should probably avoid the whole area unless you're driving a snow plow. This is no joke—you could be marooned in Buffalo.

Start at the Pennsylvania border on Route 219 north. The first leg of this trip runs around the eastern border of Allegheny State Park, the New York extension of the Allegheny National Forest. Campsites are available in and near the park, which is quite pretty, although the mountains are far from the highest in the state. The highest peaks in the southwest are around 1,300 or 1,400 feet.

For an interesting start with a difference, begin on Route 16 north towards Olean. From that road you can visit Rock City Park, with natural rock formations that will titillate your imagination.

From the Pennsylvania line, drive about eight miles to the intersection of Route 17 and take Route 17 west about seven miles to Salamanca. From Salamanca you can detour a few miles west on Route 394 to follow the Allegheny River. You'll pass the Allegheny Indian Reservation and the observation tower at Red House in the park.

Three miles west of Salamanca, or five miles east of Red House, drive north on Route 353 to Cattaraugus—about seven miles. Drive 10 miles to Dayton, and take U.S. Route 62 north to Gowanda—about four miles. You'll find the Cattaraugus Indian Reservation to the west. From there drive about 20 miles north to Hamburg.

Country roads

Genesee Gorge tour: about 20 miles through Livingston and Wyoming counties.

This drive makes a perfect partner for a trip to Pine Creek Canyon in Tioga County, Pennsylvania. Where the "Grand

Canyon of Pennsylvania" features mountain laurel and dizzyingly verdant views, the Finger Lakes' "Grand Canyon of the East" has rocky cliffs and, in general, a more rugged look. Formed by the great glaciers, this fantastic canyon caused Indians and early settlers traveling on the Genesee River to pull their boats out of the river and carry them almost 20 grueling miles along the canyon's edge. Needless to say, the going was rough, but for today's visitors, there are pleasant woodland trails from which to view the territory.

The gorge is in the middle of beautiful Letchworth State Park—14,340 acres of woods, waterfalls, and sandstone and shale cliffs. If you find yourself reluctant to leave this lovely spot, you can stay overnight at Glen Iris Inn, the former home of the park's benefactor. In 1907, William Pryor Letchworth gave 1,000 acres to the park. Today you can stay in the inn between April and November. Accommodations also are available at nearby Pinewood Lodge.

To see the park and gorge, use any of four entrances. Mt. Morris, Perry, and Portageville entrances are closed during the winter whereas the entrance at Castile is open year-round. To see the whole gorge in one continuous drive, start at the Mt. Morris entrance at the gorge's northern tip. In the 17-mile trip, stop and ramble around to see the falls. Three are considered major, with one 107 feet high. The surrounding cliffs are up to 600 feet high.

Take Route 36 about two miles northwest from Mt. Morris to the park road, a left turn. The road runs along the west bank of the river, by an overlook and Mt. Morris Dam to the High-banks Recreation Area, where there is a swimming pool, a snack bar, and an overlook.

Next is the Perry entrance, off Schenck Road at the Livingston-Wyoming County line. From the Perry entrance to the Castile entrance, you'll drive about eight miles that contain six overlooks, three picnic areas, cabins, a winter recreation area, and more.

At the southern end, you'll pass a north-to-south series of falls: Lower Falls, Middle Falls, and Upper Falls. Glen Iris Inn is in the Middle Falls area, where you will also find a statue of

Mary Jemison, "The White Woman of Genesee," a museum, and the Erie and Lackawanna Railroad tracks.

You can leave the gorge via any of Routes 436, 19A, and 38. If you prefer to take in the view from the east bank, you can take River Road between Routes 408 and 436. This road doesn't include all the overlooks and recreational areas offered on the other side, but it's not a bad drive. Be sure to note that the southern three or four miles of the road are gravel.

Finger Lakes vineyards: varied distances through Steuben, Yates, and Ontario counties.

Although California wines have come to the American viticulture forefront in quality as well as quantity, New York is still known for production of some fine wines. The grapes grown among the Finger Lakes are known for the fruity quality in wine, which some say requires a particular taste. But even if you're not a wine enthusiast at all, the vineyards and wineries are interesting. They offer the closest look Easterners will get of vineyards without going to the West Coast. Wine is in the air in the vineyard towns. It's also in the conversation and, in one case, it's even in the local luncheonette. The modest eatery actually offers a choice of 20 local wines and a champagne to go along with your burger.

The vineyards are clustered around Keuka Lake, with five sites in the town of Hammondsport, one in Naples, and one in Penn Yan.

Start in Hammondsport, which you can reach by taking Route 54 about seven miles north from the town of Bath. Take Route 54A into Hammondsport. Just before you reach the center of town, you can stop at the Taylor Wine Company, one of New York's most famous wineries. Known mainly for its dinner wines, Taylor offers tours that include a look at the 100-foot-high fermenting vats. Next door is the Great Western Wine Company, which makes champagne and other wines. A tour of the winery ends with a visit to the reception room, where you'll be served canapes, wine, and champagne—all gratis.

Drive through Hammondsport and turn left on Bully Hill

Road to go to the Bully Hill Wine Company. This is one of the best stops on the tour. The vineyard's 150 acres are perched 1,000 scenic feet above the lake banks; the land is said to be particularly fertile. This independent vineyard is run by the grandson of Taylor Wine's founder, who now produces some of the state's best wines, using unblended grapes and few machines. You can visit Bully Hill's wine shop, museum, and tasting room.

Also on Bully Hill Road is the Taylor Wine Museum on Bully Hill vineyard lands. Open between May and October, the museum is located in the buildings that housed the original Taylor Wine Company between 1883 and 1920.

Drive to the intersection of Route 77, turn left there and drive to Route 53, which will take you to the town of Naples, about 20 miles west. There you can visit the Widmer Wine Company.

Backtrack on Routes 53 and 77 and drive straight across Bully Hill Road. Turn right on Middle Road and pass the Gold Seal Winery and the Vintage Restaurant. Turn left off Middle Road, just north of the Vintage Restaurant, and then right (north) to go to Dr. Konstantin Frank's Vinifera Vineyards. Vinifera Wine Cellars, Ltd., produces quality wines, using European grafted grapes that are hand-picked. A presser, in fact, is the only machine used by the winery. Visit Vinifera just to see the gorgeously landscaped vineyards.

Another side-trip jaunt will take you north on Route 54 from Hammondsport to Penn Yan. This 23-mile tour runs around the pretty eastern banks of Keuka Lake and is worthwhile even without a destination. It also does lead you to the Boordy Wine Company vineyard, another small establishment worth seeing.

While the mileage between these sites does not add up to much, a tour of all the vineyards is done best over several days. Spend a weekend in one of the lovely area towns and you'll feel really renewed when you return to whatever you were trying to escape.

SOUTHERN NEW YORK (The Catskills and Long Island)

Scenic drives

Hawk's Nest Drive (Route 97):   about 67 miles through Orange, Sullivan, and Delaware counties. From Port Jervis to Hancock—driving the craggy cliffs of the northern Delaware River.

Following the Delaware River north of the water gap tours in Pennsylvania and New Jersey, Route 97 takes you on a breathtaking scenic drive over a mountain area. The wild banks of the Pennsylvania side give great views on a clear day, and the Catskills on the New York side offer a wealth of side trips.

Start in the cornerstone town of Port Jervis and drive three miles north on Route 97. There you'll follow Hawk's Nest Drive above rocky cliffs that rise hundreds of feet above the river and draw hawks and other wildlife to their isolated heights. This is the river gateway to the Sullivan County Catskills.

Drive two miles north and cross the bridge over the Mongaup River. Between there and Lackawaxen—about 14 miles north—you'll pass the "Eddy" towns of New York and the wilds of Pennsylvania. Pass Knights Eddy, Pond Eddy, and Handsome

Take the Hawk's Nest Drive to this replica of historic Fort Delaware. The original 1754 fort was built by settlers for protection against Indian attacks. *(Photo courtesy of Sullivan County Publicity and Tourism Department)*

Eddy to the Roebling Suspension Bridge at Minisink Ford. Built across the Delaware in 1848, the steel suspension bridge is the oldest type in the country; it was the prototype for the newer Brooklyn Bridge. Also in the Lackawaxen area is the Minisink Battlefield Memorial Park. Off Route 97, this park offers Revolutionary War history and picnic areas.

Drive 11 miles north to Narrowsburg, where you'll find Fort Delaware, and 22 miles north to Long Eddy. There you enter Delaware County, and it's 14 miles to Hancock, where the East Branch of the Delaware River breaks off and heads into the Catskills.

The New York Quickway (Route 17): about 140 miles through Orange, Sullivan, Delaware, and Broome counties. From Bear Mountain to Binghamton—a breezy look at New York's southern mountains and farmland.

The New York Quickway, which crosses the entire east-to-west width of the state, is really just that. An efficient route meant to save time, it really is not a back road, and since Route 97 can serve as an alternate route for part of its length, it almost doesn't count as a scenic route here either. The route's main feature is that it provides access to many of the unchanged communities of the southern Catskills. Route 17 is really scenic only here and near Jamestown in the state's far southwestern corner. For details on Sullivan County stops off Route 17, see below.

Southern Catskills tour: about 65 miles through Sullivan County. From Livingston Manor to Liberty—overlooks, quiet mountain drives, and quaint villages.

Although Sullivan County does not possess the Catskill's highest peaks nor its most popular resorts, it does give you a cool mountain tour. Some of the areas listed below also are likely to be less crowded than the territory of the Concords and the Grossingers.

Start your tour at Livingston Manor—Exit 96 off the Quickway (Route 17)—a nice, old resort town to visit. Return to Route 17 and go south to Exit 100 at the town of Liberty, about 9 miles. From Liberty, take Route 55 east to Neversink Reservoir. The dam on this pretty lake has several overlook spots from which to view the area. Drive five miles to Curry and turn left on the county road to Claryville, about five miles north. This is a really unspoiled mid-eighteenth-century village in the

Willowemoc covered bridge is one of five such bridges still standing in the Sullivan County Catskills. The forty-three-foot bridge spans Willowemoc Creek, two miles west of Willowemoc off Route 17. Built in 1860, it was cut in half and transported to its present location in 1913.
(Photo courtesy of Sullivan County Publicity and Tourism Department)

southern sector of Catskill Park. Backtrack halfway to Curry and stop at Halls Mills covered bridge, which crosses the Neversink.

Drive about three miles east on Route 55 to Grahamsville, a pleasant village of Quaker origin. From Grahamsville, take Route 55 around Rondout Reservoir for a scenic jaunt, and then follow the opposite bank of the lake via Route 55A back to Grahamsville, about 18 miles altogether.

Take Route 42 about six miles south from Grahamsville to Woodbourne. At that town, take Route 52 eight or nine miles west, past Loch Sheldrake to Liberty.

For scenery seekers and drivers of other persuasions, the Catskill Mountains have too many worthy routes to describe here. You might try one of the following trips if you have an extended stay in the resort area.

Route 30 can be followed along the East Branch of the Delaware River from Harvard in Delaware County to Dunraven—32 miles. Route 28 southeast from Margaretville in Delaware County to Phoenicia in Ulster County takes you by Belleayre Mountain Ski Center and other mountainside sights. The 3,590-foot Balsam Mountain to the south is a good example of the sights on this 21-mile jaunt. Finally, you can take Route 214 from Phoenicia to Tannersville on Route 23A. This is about 13 miles and offers such sights as Devil's Tombstone and Haines Falls.

Besides the generally scenic routes, there are many other routes of interest through the Catskills, following former Indian trails or historic paths. For instance, you can follow the old Shawangunk Trail—Route 52 from Newburgh into the Catskills. The Minnewaska Trail follows Routes 44 and 55 from Poughkeepsie, whereas the Onteora Trail can be traveled over Route 28 from Kingston. The Rip Van Winkle Trail goes over Route 23A from Catskill—along this route you might hear the legendary thunder of the mountain people's bowling balls. Finally, there is the Mohican Trail—Route 23 from Catskill. Any of these can provide an hour or a day of mountain air and a refreshing escape.

Montauk Highway (Route 27A and 27): about 50 miles through Suffolk County. From Westhampton to Montauk Point—beaches, windmills, mansions, and lighthouses in New York City's summer playground.

This tour covers the eastern end of Long Island and really is meant to be taken only during fall, winter, or early spring. In other words, avoid the tourist season, or this won't seem like a country road at all. If you do travel during the off-season, you'll feel that you have Long Island all to yourself—you and the ghosts of the fishermen, pirates, rumrunners, and wealthy summer residents who have flocked to this island over the centuries.

Start on Route 27A in Westhampton, the "beatnik" haven of the Hamptons—five towns that stretch along Long Island's south shore. The severe hurricane of 1938 destroyed huge summer homes along Westhampton's beach, although the town itself weathered the storm unscathed. The town also is famous for Thomas Edison's sojourn there. In the 1880s the inventor performed some of his electricity experiments at Westhampton.

Take Montauk Highway (Route 27A) about nine miles east to Hampton Bays, the fishing center of the Hamptons. Cross the channel that connects Shinnecock Bay off the south shore and Great Peconic Bay to the north. A popular calm-water swimming spot today, Shinnecock Bay was a favorite spot of the Prohibition era rumrunners on the island. The inlet visible on the ocean beach was created naturally by the 1938 hurricane. About five miles east of Hampton Bays, you'll reach Southampton College (on the left), where you can see one of the island's many old windmills.

Drive about three miles to Southampton, the gem of the Hamptons and the playground of the rich. To see some of the truly amazing "cottages" owned by summer vacationers, turn right on Flying Point Road from Route 27 (which is Hampton Road in Southampton). At the end of Flying Point Road, bear left on Dune Road, which runs east over the ocean beach bordering Mecox Bay. There you'll drive by a fascinating mixture of well-kept and well-guarded mansions and the crumbling ruins of abandoned estates. The architecture is of a variety to rival Europe's oldest cities, with colonial mansions next door to cantilever homes. One of the modern structures is a series of natural wood boxes connected by covered tunnel-type hallways. Another—one of my favorites—is an old pale-pink stucco manse, probably built around the 1920s and obviously unoccupied for quite some time. The ivy-covered walls are crumbling slightly, and the house, which is set far from the road near the dunes, is being overcome by dune grasses. It looks like something straight out of a Gothic mystery novel and inspires all kinds of fantasies about its past.

Drive east on Route 27 to Bridgehampton, about six miles. You can see the bridge that gave this town its name by turning right on Ocean Avenue, passing the windmill near Green Street, and turning left on Bridge Lane.

From Bridgehampton, take Route 27 about six miles east to East Hampton. This town is a must-see. If you have no time to stop at the other Hamptons, whiz through East Hampton anyway. The town not only has more old windmills than any other town in the United States, it also has been distinguished by a *National Geographic* Magazine panel of experts as having the most beautiful Main Street in the country. See it for yourself.

Drive another three miles east to Amagansett. This is another pretty town, and here you begin to feel extra salt in the air— you're getting close to the point. North, about two miles off the shore from Gardiner's Bay, is Gardiner's Island. This fascinating landmass has been owned by the Gardiner family since 1639.

Pass the little town called Promised Land, so-called because years ago Congress set aside land on the beach there for fish factories. Today only one factory is in operation, but the town retains its hopeful tag.

Drive about six miles east to Hither Hills State Park. If you've been here before, you'll know that a visit several years later to this park could yield completely new sights. The park's 40-foot dunes move south about three feet a year, changing the entire lay of the land. East of the park you will pass some eerie island woods and Fort Pond (on your left). Next you'll pass

Lake Montauk on your left. Woods will be spread out on your right, among which you can explore the Old Montauk Association Homes designed by Stanford White in the 1880s.

Finally, you'll pass ranch lands, the 773rd Air Force Base, and the abandoned Camp Hero army base. The road ends at the parking lot at Montauk Point. Besides the lighthouse and surrounding park, you can try your hand at treasure-hunting in Money Pond. Legend has it that the famous pirate Captain Kidd dropped anchor off Montauk Point in the mid-1600s, burying treasure on the beach. Treasure hunters over the decades, unfortunately, have had no luck.

You can explore the land's-end aura of the point to your heart's content, basking in the sun or climbing in the sand. You'll gain special respect for these awesome rocks. Scores of hapless vessels have shipwrecked on them over a period of more than three centuries.

If you intend to make a weekend of it, you can stop overnight in the town of Montauk, where shops and other tourist attractions are mostly shut down for the off-season. Good accommodations and excellent in-season seafood are available year-round, however, and a stay at the famous Gurney's Inn anytime after Labor Day can be a relaxation seeker's delight.

5

Pennsylvania

Cross-state drives

Route 6 (Roosevelt Highway): 350 miles across northern Pennsylvania—Monroe, Pike, Wayne, Lackawanna, Wyoming, Bradford, Tioga, Potter, McKean, and Warren counties. From the Poconos to Allegheny National Forest—Pennsylvania's north country in the Endless Mountains.

This tour is a long haul from the Delaware Water Gap area all the way through the majestic Allegheny National Forest and on to Ohio. If you're up to a lot of driving, it makes a perfect summer or fall vacation tour, but it's even more appropriate as an alternate scenic route for cross-state drivers bound for points east or west of Pennsylvania. If you are driving a long distance and don't care how far north or south you cross the state, take Route 6. Although it certainly does not qualify as a country road, Route 6 is neither a toll road nor an interstate. For that reason alone, Roosevelt Highway has it all over the Pennsylvania Turnpike and Interstate Route 80. To make it even more attractive to pleasure drivers, the road runs through no large cities west of Scranton.

118

If you have crossed Pennsylvania many times via the turnpike or I-80, you'll enjoy the change in atmosphere that Route 6 offers. Where the gently winding turnpike offers tranquil farmland and sweeping curves, Route 6 has crisp air and cool mountain forests. The cities along the way are more like villages, and this old route connecting them curves, bends, rises, and dips its way across the Endless Mountains, the valleys, and the foothills. For outdoor vacationers, campsites abound. Water sports are emphasized at the peaceful resort areas along the road.

Starting in the well-known—and often crowded—Poconos, where lakes are tucked in everywhere among the mountains, the road takes a turn to follow the Susquehanna River for a stretch. To the west, Route 6 touches the glorious Grand Canyon of Pennsylvania, a spectacular Tioga County gorge carved out by Pine Creek. From there, you drive straight into the awesome depths of the national forest, ending magnificently at the huge Allegheny Reservoir. Past the forest, the mountains give way to foothills, and west of the reservoir to the Ohio border, Route 6 is less scenic. In keeping with the flavor of northern Pennsylvania, Crawford County is replete with large lakes, including two of the state's largest natural lakes. Route 6 is still a pleasant ride in this northeast corner.

Like the other extended drives in this book, this tour may be broken up into several shorter drives to suit your needs. And like other woodland routes in the Mid-Atlantic states, this tour probably is most rewarding visually during the peak of autumn colors in mid-October.

Start at East Stroudsburg, Monroe's county seat. Just west of the Delaware Water Gap, this city also leads to a north-south tour of that area (see *Northeast Pennsylvania*). Take Route 402 north and drive about 30 miles to the intersection of U.S. Route 6. Along the way, the views are rewarding. To the east, where lakes and Delaware River tributaries sparkle among the hills, you'll find Winona Falls and the Fernwood Ski Area. Lakes line both sides of the route—Twelve Mile Pond and Pickerel Lake to your left, Porters Lake on your right. Pass the town and lake called Peck's Pond. On your left will be High Knob—elevation

2,062. Cross U.S. Route 84 toward the Tanglewood Ski Area (west of the road) and take Route 6 west past Lake Wallenpaupack, the largest artificial lake in the state. This 12-mile behemoth covers 5,760 acres. It was built in 1926 to supply hydroelectric power and is now a popular center for water sports of all types. (To tour the lake, see details in *Northeast Pennsylvania,* page 124.)

Take Route 6 west, crossing from Pike County into Wayne, the land of 160 lakes. Those lakes dominate the atmosphere along Route 6, and you'll be hard-pressed to sort out the many Indian names—Tedyuskung Lake, Westcolang Lake, Lackawaxen River, Rinkwig Pond, Lake Quinsigomond, and the like. From Lake Wallenpaupack to the intersection of Route 652, Route 6 heads almost directly north—about seven miles—before bearing west. Between the intersection of Route 652 and the town of Carbondale, Route 6 stretches about 18 miles westward into the Moosic Mountains.

At this point, you enter the route's only large city, Scranton. West of the city, Route 6 is a divided highway for about nine miles. After the intersection of Route 11 it returns to its more countrified status.

Drive nine miles to the town of Tunkhannock, where the route picks up the path of the beautiful Susquehanna River and follows it 42 curving miles to Towanda. Leaving Towanda, Route 6 enters Bradford County and passes Mt. Pisgah—elevation 2,278—to the town of Troy. About 18 miles from Towanda, Troy is a charming village with manicured lawns and attractive homes. Between Troy and Mansfield (about 17 miles) you'll drive by scores of small farms, following a smooth rollercoaster route up and down the hills and passing peaks that reach 2,400 feet. You'll also pass a picnic area west of Sylvania on the north side of the road. If it's harvest time in Tioga County, the smell of new-mown hay on the breeze will follow you into lumber country.

Thirteen miles from Mansfield is Wellsboro, perched on a high mountain plateau, and a must for history enthusiasts. Many of the town's founders pushed west from New England, building their frontier homes in the Greek Revival style popular in those colonies. Other old touches seem to have been preserved by Wellsboro's mountain air. The streets are still lit by old gas lamps and a stately white courthouse faces a cool nineteenth-century village green. The park in the center of town is the only one in the state dedicated completely to children. It features a statue-fountain of Wynken, Blynken, and Nod—figures from the poem by Eugene Field. From Wellsboro you also have access to the 15-mile Grand Canyon (see *Northern Pennsylvania, Country roads,* page 135).

From Wellsboro to Walton, about 30 miles, Route 6 parallels Pine Creek. In between is Lyman's Run State Park which has camping facilities. The park and Denton Hill Ski Area are south of Route 6 as is Denton Hill State Park (no camping facilities).

In Potter County you can stop at the interesting Pennsylvania Lumber Museum on the north side of the road. Ten miles west of Galeton and 10 miles east of Coudersport, the museum's exhibits tell the story of the nineteenth-century lumber men. Outside you can see a reconstructed 1890s logging camp, complete with bunkhouse, mess hall, laundry, blacksmith shop, and an authentic Shay locomotive.

If you are a hiker, you'll be interested in the Susquehannock Trail System, which you have direct access to from Route 6. Just a mile or two west of the museum is Northern Gateway near Potato City. The 85-mile loop trail forges south into the forest, where there are large numbers of state parks offering camping facilities and other wilderness attractions.

Ten miles east is Coudersport, Potter's county seat. Drive about 27 miles west to Smethport, McKean's county seat. Known as the Seneca Highlands, this beautiful region is full of back roads winding through the forest (see *Northern Pennsylvania,* page 133). South of Smethport are Devil's Den, a 2,263-foot mountain, and the McKean County fairgrounds. Toward Mt. Jewett Route 6 runs along Marvin Creek about 16 miles from Smethport. On the edge of Mt. Jewett is McKean Forest, with a roadside rest on the left side of the road.

About three miles west of Mt. Jewett is the town of Lantz Corners, gateway to the national forest. After driving eight miles on Route 6 through that dense woodland, you'll reach the town of Kane. An interesting landmark is the Kane Chapel, built in 1878 by Civil War hero and humanitarian General Thomas Kane. The Gothic-style stone church is really lovely and now is run by the Church of the Latter Day Saints. Also in Kane is a nineteenth-century Pennsylvania railroad station, typical of the depot structures of the era.

Southeast of Kane is Seneca Spring, a small spring which attracted health seekers during the seventeenth and eighteenth centuries. This was a popular stopping point on the main Indian trail from Onondaga to the Ohio River and the Carolinas. Indian forts also were said to have been built southwest of Kane during the seventeenth and eighteenth centuries, but few ruins are left to indicate their exact location.

Drive 10 miles west to Ludlow, passing Wildcat Park. From Ludlow to Warren, Route 6 runs about 20 miles through Allegheny National Forest. Altogether this route runs through 31 miles of the forest, and there are more scenic routes you can take (see *Northern Pennsylvania, Country Roads,* page 135). Just before you come to the city of Warren, you will cross the Allegheny Reservoir. If you are sightseeing, this scenic spot is a good point to end your Route 6 trip, but if you have to continue to the Ohio border anyway, Route 6 is pleasant although not as scenic in this portion of the state. As an alternate westward route from Warren, you can take U.S. Route 62 southwest from Warren to Oil City and Route 322 from Oil City to Meadsville and on to Ohio.

NORTHEASTERN PENNSYLVANIA (Honeymoon Haven)

Scenic drives

Routes 209 and 611:   about 50 miles through Pike and Monroe counties. The Delaware Water Gap, Pennsylvania style—a beautiful drive from the junction of three states, past cascading waterfalls to the gorgeous gap.

This sister tour to the New Jersey drive through the Kittatinny Mountain range offers natural and historic attractions equal to those of its eastern twin. In place of the Kittatinny Mountains, the Pennsylvania side of the Delaware River Valley is bounded by the Pocono foothills. It seems inexplicably appropriate to drive this route from north to south, which does enable you to hook up with scenic Route 6 (see *Cross-state drives*), or a tour of the Poconos (see page 124).

Start at the junction of New York, New Jersey, and Pennsylvania, in Port Jervis, New York. Take Route 209 south about seven miles to Milford. To cross into New Jersey, you can take the toll bridge at Milford. The beach at this spot is the put-in point for Delaware River paddlers. About four miles south is the first of many spectacular waterfalls that sparkle and splash in the mountain color. Raymondskill Falls is closely followed by the well-known Dingmans and Silver Thread Falls, two quite different waterfalls that tend to attract lots of visitors during the summer. South of the falls is Dingmans Ferry; another toll bridge crosses the river to New Jersey. South of Dingmans Ferry you'll pass Sky's Edge Environmental Center, one of many such outdoor programs set in the relatively undisturbed mountain communities.

At another site, Pocono Environmental Education Center, students spend a few weeks studying the stages of natural plant succession they can observe in the area—the pine and hardwood trees, lakes, streams, and waterfalls. Without participating in the live-in program, you can pause there to stroll one of the center's nature walks.

At Bushkill, you can stop off to see Bushkill Falls—100 feet of water pouring into a scenic gorge. Your next stop could be at Hidden Lake, a water recreation spot in the Marshalls Creek area. Look for the sign indicating a left turn to the lake. You can take advantage of the park's hiking trails, picnic areas, snowmobile trails, and wildlife observation. Whitetail deer, hawk, black bear, bald eagle, copperheads, and rattlesnakes abound near the lake.

Next is Smithfield Beach, another water recreation area, and the take-out point for canoes. Near Shawnee Island, turn left off Route 209 to River Road, and then take Route 611 from the borough of Delaware Water Gap to any of the three overlooks at the gap area: Resort Point, Point of Gap, or Arrow Island. If you would rather have an inland view of the south gap area, follow back roads from the borough. First, take Cherry Valley Road south, then turn left on Totts Gap Road. Finally, turn left on Mountain Road and circle back to the Delaware Water Gap.

Poconos circle tour: about 125 miles through Monroe, Pike, and Carbon counties. A string of lakes and mountains—an up-and-down scenic drive past Pennsylvania's ski slopes and honeymoon resorts.

The Poconos have attracted thousands of happy honeymooners for decades, and the land's built-in recreation facilities do attract crowds. Spring and summer seem to be the honeymooner's seasons. Winter is reserved for avid skiers and drivers with the confidence to brave the hilly roads during the snow months. Again, fall is a natural season for panoramas in these eastern Pennsylvania peaks.

Once again, Stroudsburg is the starting point as the mountain gap area continues to yield the way to westbound travelers. From the city, take Route 447 north about 15 miles to Canadensis at the intersection of Route 390. On the way, you'll pass one of many ski regions—Mount Airy, Timber Hill, and Pocono Manor.

North of Canadensis are Buck Hill Falls and the Buck Hill Family Ski Area. From Canadensis, take Route 390 north. You'll pass typical Pocono lakes on the jaunt to the intersection of U.S. Route 84, about 13 miles away. For recreational facilities, try Promised Land Lake, especially for camping and picnics.

On the other side of Route 84, take Route 507 (a left turn) south around the banks of Lake Wallenpaupack and past the seaplane base at Mountain Bay. Drive about four miles south to Newfoundland and take Route 191 south along Wallenpaupack Creek. Follow Route 191 to Route 423 past South Sterling. From Route 423 you can reach Tobyhanna State Park. Here are 4,200 acres of woodlands with two large lakes, zigzagging streams, and facilities for swimming, fishing, boating, and camping.

Continue to the intersection of Route 611—about 14 miles from Newfoundland—and drive about five miles on it to Mount Pocono. This is a popular resort area, so if you are trying to avoid crowds, skip this short leg. Take Route 940 west, which runs parallel to Interstate Route 80 for a short length and provides a scenic alternative to that highway. On both sides of the road are ski resorts and parks.

Between Mount Pocono and the town of East Side, you'll drive 25 to 30 miles of scenic territory. On the north side of the road are Jack Frost Ski Area and the Francis E. Walter Dam and Reservoir. To the south, and south of I-80, are Big Pocono State Park (no camping) and Camelback Ski Area.

At East Side, cross Interstate 80 (a left turn) to Route 534. Take Route 534 southeast about eight miles to the intersection of the Northeast Extension of the Pennsylvania Turnpike. Along the way you'll pass Hickory Run State Park, where you can camp overnight.

On the other side of the turnpike extension, past Big Boulder Ski Area to the north, take Route 534 past Split Rock Ski Area and the Pennsylvania Forest Reservoir. Driving in between Pohopoco Mountain and Weir Mountain, you'll reach the intersection of Route 209, which you can take east to return to Stroudsburg or the Delaware Water Gap.

Country roads

To anyone who has ever driven through the Poconos, just about all the roads are country roads that connect mountain with mountain, lake with lake, and mountain with lake. History is not the strong point of this area. You should find its natural beauty sufficient to make a return trip. If you're looking for shorter routes than the ones listed above, try exploring the northeast section of the county near one or more of the more remote ski areas, such as Elk Mountain or Sno Hill. Just start at the slopes and drive around beautiful Wayne County lake country.

SOUTHEAST PENNSYLVANIA (Reflection of the Past)

Scenic drives

Brandywine Valley tour: about 90 miles through Chester County. From East Branch to West Branch—following a 60-mile historic river, with stops at eight-sided schoolhouses, covered bridges, mills, and some unique barns.

If you try to compare Brandywine Creek with the mighty Delaware, the super-long Susquehanna, or even capricious Pine Creek, you may be disappointed. Next to the great rivers that run through the state, this narrow, 60-mile waterway seems small and insignificant, hardly deserving the term *river.* Navigable mainly by canoe, the lovely little river is famous for its role. in the Revolutionary War and for the waterpower it supplied during the early industrial age. At its nineteenth-century industrial peak, the Brandywine had more than 130 mills standing along its banks, but only a few are left for us to see.

Local residents might tell you the river is named for a Dutch gin, Brandewijn. As the story goes, a gin-laden ship accidentally dumped its cargo into the Brandywine estuary, giving the creek its somewhat yellowish tinge. A less imaginative recounting says the town's name came from an early Swedish settler named Brantwyn.

The tour is easily broken into a northern and southern leg. Surrounding attractions are centered on the two branches of the river. Even if you don't stop at any of the historic sites, you'll see hundreds of old mill-era houses in passing.

Start the tour in West Chester, the county seat. Sometimes called the Athens of Pennsylvania for its Greek Revival buildings, it is easily accessible from Philadelphia. From the town, take Route 162 west, passing several historic homes on the way to Route 322. Turn north (right) on Route 322 and drive along the East Branch of the Brandywine River. Route 322 is an old lake-to-sea route that still guides travelers from Erie to Atlantic City. Here it is called Downingtown Road. Just east of the road, watch for anglers fishing in Valley Creek, which is stocked with trout.

Drive a few miles north to Harmony Hill Road, where you'll find Gibson's Bridge, one of 17 covered bridges in Chester County. Built in 1872, the 78-foot bridge was named after George Gibson, a local farmer. From here north the creek used to be somewhat polluted, but thanks to local efforts, the quality of the water has improved in recent years.

Drive to Downingtown, an early East Branch industrial center. In Kerr Park along the river you will see a 1710 loghouse, adorned with colorful windowboxes of flowers.

North of Downingtown the road turns into Route 282. A mile or two north, near Dorlan, you will pass the Shryock Brothers' establishment. One of the oldest continuously used paper mills in the country, this mill assists the river cleanup effort by recycling its own waste water.

Drive a short distance to Marsh Creek State Park, where there is a 535-acre reservoir that provides fishing and boating for visitors and flood control for area residents. To reach the park, turn right on Lyndell Road from the town of that name. In the park's northern sector you can cross Larkin Bridge, a 60-foot covered bridge built in 1881. Originally erected over Marsh Creek, the bridge was moved when the lake was formed in 1972. You'll find it over a small creek about a quarter of a mile off the road.

A few miles north on Route 282 is Springton, where you can visit Springton Manor, built on land granted to the original owners by William Penn. The next town you will pass is Glenmore, a pleasant village with attractive Victorian houses.

Take Route 282 across Route 82 and drive straight on Wyebrook Creek Road. Turn right on Bollinger Road to the interesting Isabella Furnace. This old stone structure, operated by the Potts family until the early 1900s, is being restored.

Turn left on Woods Drive and left again on Isabella Road. Turn right on Potts Road, and right again to Struble Lake, which has the oldest of the East Branch dams. This dam also provides water recreation and flood control.

Turn left on Fontaine Road to Welsh Hills—this is headwaters territory, the source of the East and West Branch waters. From here, turn left on Talbotville Road and right on School

Road. You'll enter the center of Amish and Mennonite farm country, as picturesque here as it is throughout all of southern and southeastern Pennsylvania. Continue on School Road, staying to the right to turn off on Todd Road. Turn left on Route 10 and left back onto Route 322 at Honeybrook. This delightful borough, called Waynesburg, was settled by the Welsh.

Drive about five miles south on Route 322 to Icedale. Icedale Lake is a public fishing hole, so-named because it used to supply ice to local cities. Turn right on Route 82, right again on Knoll Road and across the railroad tracks and West Branch to Cedar Road. Turn left on Martin's Corner Road and drive through Hibernia Park. Formerly an ironmaster's home, this 700-acre estate has a beautiful mansion and offers camping and picnicking to visitors.

Turn left when you hit the railroad tracks again and turn right on Cedar (crossing the railroad tracks and river again). Turn right on Hibernia Road—the old farm road to Wagontown—and you'll pass the ruins of the Hibernia ironworks. Houses and an old drover's inn nearby are being restored.

Cross the railroad tracks and West Branch once again and turn left on Route 340 at Wagontown. Turn right on Route 82. South of Route 30 there are slopes covered with the pink blossoms of crown vetch, a groundcover planted to prevent soil erosion.

Continue on Route 82 to Coatesville, an industrial town, and drive south across the tracks and river to Youngsburg Road. Turn left on Strasburg Road, another old drover's route running from Lancaster County to Philadelphia, passing Mortonville Oak and an old log cabin. Cross the inevitable railroad tracks and river again, and turn right on Laurel Road at Mortonville. Near the point where the West Branch and Buck and Doe Run meet, you'll find the ruins of a unique type of barn once built throughout the area. Only the barn walls are standing, but they show the strange conical supports that were used in this Chester County style.

Turn right on Branch Creek Road, along which you'll pass the remnants of the area's original vast hemlock forest. At Embreeville, turn left on Route 162 east. Along the way you'll pass the

Star Gazer's stone, an indication of the point where Mason and Dixon began their 1764 survey of Pennsylvania and Maryland.

In Marshallton, a beautifully restored 1700s village, you can check out 200-year-old Marshallton Inn. Drive to the intersection of Route 322 and take Creek Road south to Copes Bridge. Built in 1806, this is a triple-arched stone bridge. South of it, note the river floodplains. This is the end of the northern section of the Brandywine Valley tour.

To begin the southern leg, continue south and turn right on Route 842. You'll pass both branches of the creek, more floodplains, and an area of contour strip farming. Drive a total of about five miles to Unionville at Route 162. This historic settlement was a stopping point on the old farmers' route to the Philadelphia markets.

Take Route 82 west of Unionville to Doe Run, about five miles. There's another covered bridge over Buck Run. Turn left on Springdell-Doe Run Road, driving through a 10,000-acre farm with 2,000 Gertrudis steers. You'll also see old Blow Horn Mill. From this cattle and horse area, turn left on Touron Road and left again on Maple Grove Road. Turn right on Ryan Road and right again on Clonmell-Upland Road. Then turn left on Route 841 and stop for a picnic at Primitive Hall, a gorgeous brick Georgian mansion built in 1738.

Turn left on Route 926 east, called Street Road, which was laid out by William Penn himself. On this historic road you'll pass one of the many Quaker meeting houses in the area—the London Grove Friends Meeting, built of white oak and dating back to William Penn's time.

Turn right on Walnut Road toward Longwood. The area you drive through is a mushroom-growing region. Turn left on Longwood Road to the intersection of Route 52. There you'll find famous—and sometimes crowded—Longwood (botanical) Gardens, with its lily pools and seasonal floral displays. Continue to Hamorton Road and drive a few miles to the Brandywine Battlefield area near Route 100. Turn left (north) on Route 100 where you'll find Chadds Ford, a historic village with the Brandywine River museum—the John Chadd House, the Chris Sanderson Museum, and battlefield park.

Turn right at Brinton's Bridge Road to Dilworthtown. Turn right on Oakland Road to the stone house, built in 1704. On its grounds are an herb garden and several out buildings. The house is furnished with many authentic pieces. Backtrack to Brinton's Bridge Road and turn left on Birmingham Road. Another Quaker church, the Birmingham Friends Meeting was established in 1690 and served as a hospital for troops from both sides during the Brandywine Battle. Of special interest is the eight-sided schoolhouse on its grounds.

Backtrack again and turn right on Wylie Road. Then turn right on Route 100, back to the intersection of Route 52. If you like roller coasters and bumper cars, you can end your trip at the modern amusement park nearby.

Country roads

Route 562:   about 15 miles through Berks County.

The city of Reading is right in the center of picturesque Pennsylvania Dutch country. Almost any of the secondary highways that radiate from it lead to a land of tranquil farms and rolling foothills. Reading is sixty miles northwest of Philadelphia, and it has some strange sights. Sometimes called the "Factory Outlet Capital of the U.S.A.," Reading and its suburbs draw thousands of bargain seekers to the partially face-lifted warehouses on the 1100 block of downtown Moss Street. There shoppers revel in the piles of clothing, housewares, and other merchandise sold at wholesale prices. Its other claims to fame include possession of the streetcar named "Desire," a full-sized pagoda perched on the mountain that overlooks the city, and its own little skyline drive, called Duryea Drive.

Outside Reading there are several Amish farms open for public tours, but these *are* the tourist spots and a more interesting trip to this region can be made by driving the country roads away from the public places. Almost any drive will give you views of the world-renowned red farm buildings, with their steadfast barns and colorful hex signs, and an occasional horse-and-buggy transporting a family of the famous Amish people.

This is a perfect cameo of Amish life in Lancaster County—farmer and son drive their horse and buggy past a typical one-room schoolhouse in Pennsylvania Dutch country.
(Photo courtesy of Pennsylvania Dutch Tourist Bureau)

Route 562 is a secondary highway that runs from Reading. From Stonersville to Boyertown, the trip totals about 15 miles, but you can extend it by taking side trips as your whims dictate.

Take Route 562 east out of Reading. If you choose to skip the city entirely, aim for a launching point near Stonersville, where the scenery becomes more natural. From that area you can visit the Daniel Boone Homestead, although it is a popular tourist site. Route 562 is an old highway, linking miniscule villages with names like Yellow House and Bird in Hand. Also called the Oley Valley Turnpike, the road rolls by these towns before you notice them. Drive at a leisurely pace and watch for the old stone springhouse on the side of the road. It has a large stone basin from which you can sample the water.

End your tour of Route 562 at Boyertown. In 1763 this town was noted for its buggy-building business. Later, citizen Duryea built the first horseless carriage there. You can take in this bit of automotive history via the museum in the Boyertown Auto Body Works.

Route 23 to Valley Forge National Historical Park: just a few green miles through Chester County.

Valley Forge is hardly a little-known site, but the green, hilly land surrounding the park is well worth the sacrifice of solitude. The roads through the Valley Forge-King of Prussia area are unpredictable, narrow and winding. Watch out for hazardous conditions during winter. If extended from the park, Route 23 makes a good scenic drive west to the Pottstown area.

To reach the park, take Route 23 all the way in or get off the Pennsylvania Turnpike at the Valley Forge interchange. In the park are many historic points of interest, but it is the back road side trips that lead to the least commercial sites. If you don't mind crowds, explore Washington's 1777-78 headquarters, the restored mill that once ground grain for the general's troops, and the modern, all-weather theater.

Leave the park via Route 252 south and turn right on Yellow Springs Road. There you'll find Knox Bridge, built in 1865 and reconstructed in 1960. This 66-foot bridge across Valley Creek is the most frequently painted and photographed of all the county covered bridges, possible because of its location. Named for Henry Knox, the first U.S. Secretary of War under President Washington, the bridge is next door to the house that served as Knox's Valley Forge headquarters.

A popular subject of Pennsylvania painters and photographers, Knox Bridge crosses Valley Creek on the outskirts of Valley Forge State Park, Chester County.

From the bridge, head west toward Diamond Rock Hill Road. Just before its intersection you'll find the Diamond Rock eight-sided schoolhouse. From there, turn right on Diamond Rock Hill Road to extend your trip to a visit to the Warton Esherick Museum (on the right).

NORTHERN PENNSYLVANIA (The Endless Mountains)

Scenic drives

Allegheny National Forest tour: about 130 miles through McKean, Warren, and Forest counties. From Kinzua Dam to Heart's Content—winding deep into the primeval forest, from overlooks to picnic groves.

If you like the profound calm of virgin woodlands, you will appreciate this drive, one of the most scenic in the Mid-Atlantic States. Most of the stopping points are intended to help you absorb the atmosphere rather than retrace important moments in American history. You don't have to drive more than half a mile on this tour before you learn respect and love for this forest. And if you find the forest so tempting you can't stand to stay in your car, you can make a day-long outing of this trip, ending a short section of the drive at one of the many recreation areas or picnic spots.

Start in McKean County, just east of the national forest's edge, at the town of Mt. Jewett. From that woodside town, take Leg. Route 42044, six or seven miles northeast to the Kinzua Bridge. This stark viaduct, built in 1883, was erected over the Kinzua Valley by the Erie & Lackawanna Railroad. Upon its completion, it was touted as everything from the highest bridge in the world to the eighth wonder of the world. Kinzua, the name of an ancient Indian village that used to be nearby, comes from an Indian word meaning "they gobble." "They" in this case meant the wild turkeys that are just one of the abundant species of wildlife still found here.

Continue north on Route 42044 to Route 59. Turn left on Route 59 and drive about eight miles to Lafayette at the edge of

Called everything from the eighth wonder of the world to the world's highest bridge when it was built, Kinzua Viaduct is off Route 59, near majestic Allegheny National Forest.
(Photo courtesy of McKean County Planning Commission)

the forest. A mile north is Timbuck and from there to Warren, Route 59 travels 29 miles through the forest.

Near the forest's western border the road crosses Allegheny Reservoir. On the lake's eastern border is Rimrock Overlook, for views of boaters on the Kinzua Branch of the reservoir; picnic tables are nearby, and a beach is available to swimmers. Cross the reservoir to Jake's Rocks, another overlook, with wooded trails leading to high points in the forest. For campers, there is Dewdrop Campground. On a side trip, you can take Route 262 north (the Longhouse Scenic Drive around the reservoir).

On the western edge of the reservoir is Kinzua Dam, 2,000 feet of concrete and earthwork that form the lake. From the dam, drive six miles west to Warren, then six miles to U.S. Route 62. Drive about 15 miles south on Route 62, along the Allegheny River. You'll reach the little village of Tidioute, almost a miniature community, and turn left (east) on Route 337 from the town. About eight miles east, at Sandstone Springs, turn right on Forest Route 18. Along that road you'll pass

Heart's Content, a 120-acre preserve of giant white pines. Many of them are hundreds of years old. No new pines have been planted there in more than 160 years. Nature trails and picnic and camping areas are across the street. The Wheeler Lookout Tower, one of six in the forest, also is nearby.

Take Route 18 to Sheffield, and turn right on Route 948-666. Along that route is Tionesta Scenic Area, 2,000 acres of virgin hemlock and beech trees. Bear right to stay on Route 666, which follows Tionesta Creek. To the east is an area full of springs—Blue Jay, Porter Farm, and Amsler among them. Take Route 666 back to Route 62—about 35 miles—and take Route 62 north about seven miles, back to Tidioute.

McKean County tours: scenic routes of varying lengths through a woodland county. From gamelands to forest and backcountry roads and peaceful wilderness.

McKean County, proud of its inclusion in the Allegheny National Forest, is now designating scenic routes throughout its lands, inside and outside the forest boundaries. As of 1977, Route 59 was the only officially designated scenic route, but many more are on the boards for the same honor.

Through the forest section of the county, you can take Route 321 from the town of Kane to the intersection of Route 346 along Willow Creek. Route 346 also is slated for designation as a scenic route, and you can drive it southeast from Willow Bay near the New York border to Bradford.

In the southern and eastern portions of the county, outside the national forest, you can try Route 46 from Smethport to the gamelands south of Betula. Or drive Route 146 from Route 46 to Marvindale. Another county road, from Clermont to Five-Mile Run at the Elk County border, also is being considered as a scenic route. By the time you drive these roads, they may be marked as self-guiding tours.

Country roads

Pennsylvania's Grand Canyon: about 15 miles through Tioga County.

Arizona's sister canyon in Pennsylvania is an awesome sight for Easterners. Cutting into the Endless Mountains in wild Tioga County, pristine Pine Creek winds 1,000 feet below the surrounding peaks, providing a fantastic float route for paddlers of all kinds and a spectacular, if short, drive for sightseers.

This is Pennsylvania mountain territory at its best, with the rhododendron and laurel so thick on the undulating terrain that the state holds its annual laurel festival here every June. The area also is part of a designated fall foliage tour of Pennsylvania that is just as colorful, but in a more vibrant range. This is real wilderness territory, so if you're taking a transportation means more primitive than auto, be sure to watch out for the rattlesnakes that sun themselves in the open brush areas. On the same note, don't try canoeing unless you are sure of your ability. Although Pine Creek is not a terribly rough waterway, neither is it as placid as a lake.

Wellsboro, the town that offers access to canyon country, has provided several color-coded arrow tours of its natural pride and joy, and you can take one of these tours from the town.

To blaze your own trail, choose one of the two main overlooks; there is one on each side of the river. For a drive down the length of the canyon, head for the west bank.

To see the whole canyon, start on Route 6 at the town of Ansonia. Drive just a quarter of a mile west to a dirt road on the left, Colton Point Road. The road winds about five miles south to Colton Point State Park—elevation 2,500 feet—which has a great overlook. From the point, you can head south by backtracking and turning left at the first fork. Bear left again at Right Branch (creek) and left again on West Rim Road, which runs all the way along the canyon. You'll be treated to about 10 miles of inspiring views of flowering laurel in spring and summer and the brilliant flame colors of the mountain trees in the fall.

You'll cross and pass creeks and runs all the way to Blackwell, at the intersection of Route 414, where the trip ends.

To take the tour and see the canyon from the east side, start on Route 660, driving southwest from Wellsboro to Leonard Harrison State Park. There is another canyon overlook there, but there is no east side road to take you all the way along the canyon. To see the area on the east, take Sullevan Road south from the park and turn left on Kennedy Road to Leg. Route 58013 (a right turn). Drive to Clay Mine Road, which runs through the area inland from the canyon and creek.

Williamsport's Skyline Drive: seven miles through Lycoming County.

One of several "little skyline drives" through Pennsylvania, this tour near the charming town of Williamsport winds around Bald Eagle Mountain. Access to the drive is from scenic U.S. Route 15 north (see *Scenic drives, Central Pennsylvania,* page) toward South Williamsport.

South Williamsport is the home of the national Little League Headquarters and the league's World Series Stadium. Pass the headquarters and, at the bottom of the hill, watch for the sign indicating Skyline Drive. Turn left at the sign on Route 554, which blazes a pleasant trail up the mountain. You'll pass an overlook at Frank Heller Reservoir; bear left just past it. The road then winds along the top of Bald Eagle Mountain, with two more overlooks to stop at. The skyline drive emerges at a roadside rest along Route 15.

Communing with the spirits: Individual trips to the ghost towns in wild and woolly Eld County.

Elk County, aptly named, is full of wildlife. Included in the Allegheny National Forest, the county has few large urban areas; flora and fauna flourish here. Unfortunately, human settlements of the lumbering and mining days did not fare well here. These ghost towns give you a rare chance to see towns that moved in the opposite direction from most of the densely populated Mid-Atlantic areas. Unlike many preserved fragments of wilderness, Elk County often seems to be ruled by its wildlife. These trips offer you a somewhat rare look at defunct human settlements amidst a land again ruled by the plants and animals.

The following is a listing of five areas with ghost towns—tiny communities, many of them of makeshift origin, that sheltered lumbermen and coal miners of the nineteenth century. All that's left of these towns is some tell-tale woodland trails, an occasional old coke oven, or the remains of a lumbering operation. History buffs should grab the chance to see these quickly disintegrating fossils of communities.

You won't find the usual Mid-Atlantic maze of highways, county routes, and country roads in Elk County, so there is no connecting route to lead you to all these ghost towns. Consequently, I have listed them as individual trips, east to west, which you can choose to visit according to your available time.

Wilmer and the elks

Start a couple of miles south of Route 120 at the Elk County corner in the middle of its eastern limit. Take Route 120 into Elk County, bearing left at any promising-looking road; or pick up Route 555 east along the Bennett Branch of the Sinnemahoning Creek. This is a really pretty area. Moss agate—and, of course, wildlife galore—has been found in the land to the south of Route 555.

Turn right at Dents Run, about five miles from the county line, and look for signs of Wilmer, a ghost town. Without straying completely from the theme, I felt compelled to include a side trip here to the game lands that are home to Pennsylvania's only elk herd.

After exploring the ghost town ruins, continue northeast, and you will come to the forest-glade area that shelters the state's elk herd, a worthwhile side trip that may give you a glimpse of the rare animals.

Glen Fisher and Coalville

Between Weedville and Caledonia on Route 555, a distance of about three miles, you'll find two ghost towns. Built strategically along the creek and the Pennsylvania and Ohio Railroad tracks, these towns were dependent upon coal. You'll find a coke oven in the ruins and a cave to the south. For a slightly bizarre side trip, head north of Weedville to Bill Smith's Rattlesnake Zoo.

Grove

Getting to this particular ghost town can be half the fun, if you're driving during May or June. Starting on Route 949, go southwest from Ridgway and keep an eye—or a nose—out for the Mill Creek area. Its acres of odiferous skunk cabbage are said to attract black bears on a daily basis during these two months. From Miller Creek, take Route 949 to Toby's Creek, just east of the town of Portland Mills. Turn left at the creek and drive about two miles to the ghost town once called Grove. For hikers, Bear's Mouth and Indian Rock Trails lead to the ruins from the left (east) side of the road.

Arroyo

From Grove, return to Route 949 and continue west from Portland Mills. Where the road forks at Beech Bottom Run (less than two miles from Portland Mills) bear right and drive about a mile and a half. There the road meets the Clarion River, a designated scenic canoe route; here you'll find the ruins of the town of Arroyo.

Corduroy and Middle Town

The last two ghost towns, in the western section of the county, probably are the most difficult to reach. They both lie along Little Hunter Creek in the middle of the national forest, about 30 miles directly east of Tionesta Reservoir. To visit the sites, take either Route 66 and bear southeast or Route 948 and bear southwest. North of the state game lands you'll find the vestiges of Corduroy and Middle Town.

CENTRAL PENNSYLVANIA (Farming, Mining and the Mighty Susquehanna)

Scenic drives

Susquehanna River tour: 80 miles and more through the Susquehanna River Valley through Cumberland, Perry, Juniata, Snyder, and Union counties (west bank drive); Dauphin, Northumberland, Montour, and Columbia counties (east bank drive). From Harrisburg to Allenwood or Bloomsburg—drive the east or west bank of the serene Susquehanna, past tidy towns, reclaimed coal fields, mountain orchards, gorges, and waterfalls.

The Susquehanna River and the land under its influence cover so much territory and include such diversity of historic and scenic attractions that it's almost impossible to describe it all. There probably are thousands of country roads and miles of scenic routes to choose from. Each one will have something slightly different to offer. To include as much of this river heritage as possible, this tour hugs the river from the state capital to the lumber country around Williamsport. Depending on your time and wishes, you can drive either the east or west bank and see basically the same sights.

U.S. Route 15 to Allenwood is the west bank drive and a major route through the area. The east bank route takes you over Route 147 and other county roads and is more primitive. It eventually leads to the mountain country of Columbia and Montour counties.

For either route, start in Harrisburg, taking U.S. Route 22 north. Cross the river at Clark's Ferry, where you can see huge stone columns that held up a covered bridge 100 years ago. Try to imagine the towpath that ran alongside it, where mules pulled canal boats across the river. This was part of the Main Canal, a 300-mile system that was the main water highway between Philadelphia and Pittsburgh.

Eighteen miles from Harrisburg, take U.S. Route 11-15 north about 10 miles to Liverpool. Follow the signs to the Millersburg ferry. The 20-minute ferry ride takes you two miles across this serene river, straight into one of Mark Twain's novels. The *Falcon* and the *Roaring Bull* have two stern paddlewheels reminiscent of the Mississippi River boats. If you ride during cold or rainy weather, you can take shelter in a rocking chair beside the wood-burning stove in the ferry's cabin. These staunch little boats carry only four cars at a time ($1.50 for car and driver) and run daily between dawn and dark, except when the Susquehanna freezes. Across the water, you'll float by scattered islands dotted with duck blinds and cottages.

When you get off the ferry, drive to the top of the hill and turn right on Route 147 to go through Millersburg. This is a worthwhile side trip, taking you past the town's old-time square and gazebo. Turn around and go north on Route 147, a total of about 30 miles to Sunbury. You'll ride through a number of charming river towns, with pleasant rural land between them. This route follows the Tulpehocken path, and Indian trail used by Iroquois chiefs carrying peace wampum to Philadelphia. Look for the old barns with fading tobacco ads painted on their sides.

Just before you reach Sunbury, take a few minutes and get out of your car to walk up the small green slope to the great wall that keeps the mighty river from pouring into Sunbury. That town, first settled by white men in 1742, was the site of three Indian villages. You can visit Edison Inn, the first building in the world commercially wired and lit by a three-wire electrical distribution system. On the north edge of town is Fort Augusta, a reproduction of the original 1756 log fort that played a role in the French and Indian and Revolutionary wars. Behind the fort is old Hunter Mansion, now a museum.

The road then crosses the North Branch of the Susquehanna to Northumberland, wedged in between two river branches. This is a charming village of flagstone walks and brick houses. In town, a block east of the bridge to Sunbury and a block south of U.S. Route 11, you can visit the Joseph Priestley house. The clapboard building, built in the Georgian Colonial style, was home to the discoverer of oxygen between 1744 and 1802.

Drive about five miles north to the point where Route 147 turns into Route 405. Drive two miles north and turn right on Route 45. In the 15 miles to Danville you'll pass more farm country. Look for an open field on the left with Sodom School, another eight-sided schoolhouse built of stone in 1836. At the plaque marking the school, you can detour right. Take the narrow road that goes down the hills and winds through the woods to one of the country's oldest covered bridges—built in 1812 at a cost of $575. This road comes out on Route 45, where you turn right and drive east to Route 642. Ten miles east of Route 405 you come to Mooresburg, home of the One-Room School Museum.

Drive about four miles east to Mausdale and turn right

(south) on Route 54 to Danville, about two miles. Here is another town square surrounded by streets of attractive frame houses. This is the former home of an imaginative fellow named Frank DeLong who invented the bobby pin, among other items.

Cross the river and pass through the town of Riverside over a mountain to Elysburg (10 miles south of Danville). From Elysburg, take Route 487 about two miles south to Paxinos. From Paxinos, follow Route 61 south into the Anthracite Coal Fields of Pennsylvania. The people in this area are particularly friendly, and you can see the landfills and saplings that are the beginnings of the reclamation of strip-mined land. In the five-mile trip to Shamokin, you'll pass coal settlements whimsically named Weight Scales, Rough and Ready, Fearnot, Hunkelbergers, No. 10 Siding, Seek, Scow, and Vade. In Shamokin you can visit the Glen Burn Mine and Colliery. On the side of the mountain, the mine and the anthracite museum (open weekends and holidays) offer guided tours and a three-mile mine buggy ride into the rock mountain tunnel.

From Shamokin, Route 61 runs about nine miles east to Mt. Carmel—more mining remains—and enters Columbia County, which has 28 covered bridges.

Four miles east of Mt. Carmel, you'll come to Centralia. Turn north on Route 42. In the 16 miles to Catawissa you'll drive over Aristes Mountain, passing Numidia and Slabtown. Catawissa, a little village hemmed in by mountains, has an old Quaker Meeting House on South Street. Between Slabtown and Newlin, take the township road off Route 422 to see a really old log cabin.

Cross the river to Bloomsburg (five miles north of Catawissa), the Columbia county seat. Orchards abound in this hilly area. Take Route 11 east to Berwick—about 13 or 14 miles northeast—and take Route 93 west past the Old Stone Church, the original North Branch Methodist Church. Drive'about 10 miles to Route 487, turn right at the stop sign, and run through charming Orangeville, Forks, and Stillwater to Benton. A side trip to your right from that town takes you to Benton Dam and Park, a beautiful spot.

From Benton drive about 10 miles north to Ricketts Glen

State Park, a fitting ending for this beautiful tour. This stunning outdoor heaven includes 13,000 acres with two branches of Kitchen Creek cutting through deep gorges, meeting at "Waters Meet," and flowing through the giant hemlocks for two miles. Some of the trees are more than 500 years old; the main attraction of the park is its 33 waterfalls, one of which is Ganoga Falls—100 feet long.

To take the west bank Susquehanna tour, start from Route 22 in Harrisburg, but don't take the ferry to Millersburg. Continue on Route 15 all the way to Allenwood. The West Branch Valley that you end up in was one of the world's most prosperous lumber centers from 1862 to 1891. Williamsport, the hub of the action, was tagged "Sawdust City" and the "City of Millionaires" by onlookers.

In Allenwood you'll find the famous federal prison farm as well as "Reptiland," a zoo full of slithery creatures. For an interesting side trip, drive north of Route 80 to the South Williamsport Skyline Drive (see *Country roads, Northern Pennsylvania*).

Country roads

The huge stretch of central Pennsylvania is dominated by farms and reclaimed coal mines. Small-town roads are an interesting combination of strip-mined lands, nineteenth-century town buildings and thriving farms that survived the mining age. The towns themselves are not always beautiful, but if you are used to flatlands, the way these towns have been nonchalantly built anywhere among the slopes will amuse you. If you're taking a long drive through central Pennsylvania, be sure to stop in at least one of the many towns to acquire some of the local farm products. The locally cured hams and bacon are some of the best I've ever tasted. And although I missed my chance to sample it many times, the local ice cream is said to rival the most delicious in the country.

Your best bet in any central county is to head out of whatever town you are in to start a scenic drive—they are available in almost any direction. Wildlife still abounds in much of this territory so drive very slowly around curves, keeping an eye out for a deer, rabbit, squirrel, or pheasant crossing the road.

Clearfield, Cambria, and Indiana counties

A nice route through these counties is Route 219, which can be traveled any distance between Spangler in Cambria County north to Dubois in Clearfield County, about a 48-mile total. Along the way you can stop at the only covered bridge over the West Branch of the Susquehanna. At the intersection of Route 36 just south of McGees Mill, this 107-foot bridge was built in 1873 of white pine and was painted red. There's a picnic grove next to it. At the cornerstone of Clearfield, Cambria, and Indiana counties the Cherry Tree Monument marks the end of the navigable stretch of the West Branch of the Susquehanna.

If you're an antique buff, the main feature of this road is the scattered antique junk shops, many of them housed in old farm buildings. Their contents often represent the gleanings from crumbled farm buildings. One of my favorites is Thelma's, a chaotic looking place run by a cheerful proprietor who has an apparent touch for acquiring the best of what's around. There are knickknacks, antique curios, and old pieces of rusty farm equipment that ambitious decorators snap up to give their houses a rustic air.

A tour through the area that offers similar attractions is Route 322 west from Clearfield to Luthersburg, followed by Route 219 to West Liberty and Route 119 to Punxsutawney. This is a 42-mile scenic route. Again, it is important to slow down almost to a stop around the numerous hairpin curves. The last time I drove through (in early spring) a whole family of deer silently flew across the road, only to disappear as quickly into the woods on the other side as they had appeared. These gazelle-like creatures give no warning of their appearance, and if we had not been driving a mere five miles per hour around that bend, we might have been the cause of their tragic death.

Schuylkill and Berks counties

Offering variety from its western neighbors, this region is

marked by slightly flatter farmland accented by sharp rocky mountains. The best example of this terrain is the route to and around Hawk Mountain Sanctuary.

This rugged peak is near the Schuylkill-Berks County line, a couple of miles north of Hamburg. Hawk Mountain rises 1,000 to 1,500 feet above wheat fields and apple trees. Its 2,000 acres are a stop along the fall migration route of hawks and eagles, who rest atop the mountain rocks. The 1,521-foot Lookout Point accessible to hikers gives a 70-mile view of the surrounding patchwork farms on a clear day.

To reach the sanctuary, take Route 78-22 west to Route 143 (north) and bear west at Albany a couple of miles to the mountain. Or take Route 61 north past Hamburg, crossing Schuylkill River and then the Little Schuylkill River. Just past the second crossing, turn right and drive three miles to Drenersville. Turn right to reach Hawk Mountain. The sanctuary headquarters is an old stone house, called Schaumboch's Tavern when it was built in 1790. From there you can wander through the second-growth birch and oak forest and see also scattered hemlock, white pine, patches of mountain laurel, and enormous rhododendrons.

West of the sanctuary are several areas worth exploring via country roads, many of which offer scenic overlook stops. Try Routes 895 and 443 between Pine Grove and Summit Station— about 10 miles each. Almost any side road in between the two east-west routes takes you on an interesting drive.

SOUTHERN PENNSYLVANIA (Battlefields and Bridges)

Truly a land of living history, southern Pennsylvania is a complex country, where past and present offset each other as naturally as the valleys complement the mountains of this beautiful territory. To the modern auto traveler, no physical divisions separate the old from the new because the relics and monuments of the eighteenth century hold their ground alongside the structures of today. Here, you'll find the last resting place of soldiers from the French and Indian, Revolutionary, and Civil wars, along with countless monuments to the tragic clashes between Indians and white settlers. You'll drive by pioneer homesteads and modern farm structures, covered bridges and modern re-sorts; you'll find a pioneer fort sharing an acre with the local gas station.

Understandably, this region of Pennsylvania draws many sightseers. Southern Pennsylvania is famous for its scenic, rec-reational, and historic attractions, which can and do draw crowds during peak seasons. Resorts abound here, as well as every type of simpler accommodation, from roadside motel to country inn. If you really like solitude, avoid the ski areas during the winter and the fishing resorts in the summer. Almost any time of year offers spectacular views, though, and if you're planning a nonstop drive across the state, there are many scenic routes available.

Scenic drives

U. S. Route 30 (Lincoln Highway): 150 miles through Adams, Franklin, Fulton, Bedford, Somerset, and Westmoreland coun-ties. From Gettysburg to Greensburg—mountain gaps and mineral springs, laurel-covered hills and coral caverns, living history, and a land of frontiers and battlegrounds.

U.S. Route 30 is especially nice for a long-distance drive if you have a little extra time to devote to your surroundings. It's a great alternative to the Pennsylvania Turnpike for east-west trips and is literally lined with sightseeing spots. Depending upon the season and the weather, you can find the less crowded sites and still absorb quite a bit of Americana. And if you're interested in a particular period of history or one type of structure, check the sites listed below ahead of time and map out a selective tour of like attractions.

For Revolutionary War buffs, there's Fort Loudon, the John Bourns House, and the town named after Dr. Hugh Mercer, Washington's Revolutionary War surgeon. Civil War museums, battlegrounds, and monuments also are scattered throughout the area, ranging from the spectacular Gettysburg to more intimate local relics. For those interested in the pioneer days, there are poignant reminders of the clashes and the peaceful encounters

(Above) One of Gettysburg's covered bridges, Sauk's Bridge, is near the Eisen-
hower farm. (Below) Confederate cannon along Seminary Ridge, Gettysburg.
(Photos courtesy of Gettysburg Travel Council)

between Indians and white men. And for those who can't spare
the time to drink in all this history, southern Pennsylvania offers
regal mountains and mountain gaps, the fertile Cumberland
Valley, a little Skyline Drive, and the beautiful colors and scents
of blossoming laurel, rhododendron, apple, and peach trees.
Gettysburg seems like a natural starting point for this 150-mile
tour through history. The Gettysburg National Military Park
and National Cemetery lie in a hilly, green area, and offer at
least a day's worth of sightseeing to undertake on foot. Gettysburg is a popular place, so if you don't like grand-scale tourist
attractions, skip it.

From Gettysburg, drive west on Route 30 through this pleasant mountain-gap territory. The surrounding peaks reach almost 2,000 feet, and the trees are gorgeous in the fall. You'll find
Caledonia State Park at the intersection of Route 233; there you
can pick up the Frontier Trail, sponsored by the Franklin
County Tourist Council. Tracing a wide circle around Chambersburg, this auto trail is marked with yellow and blue signs to
guide drivers, and encompasses a wide variety of interesting
sites.

Besides the famous battlefield, Gettysburg, Pennsylvania has the Miniature
Horse Farm, where the largest North American herd of fourteen- to thirty-six-
inch-high Falabella miniature horses can be seen.

Near Caledonia, just south of Route 30, hikers can hook up with the famous Appalachian Trail. Also at Caledonia is Thaddeus Stevens' Blacksmith Shop, where summer visitors may watch the smithy operation as it was performed during the Civil War days. This shop was the only building left standing after the Confederate Army burned the immediate area in 1863 in anticipation of the battle at Gettysburg.

From Caledonia, drive about 10 miles west to Chambersburg. In Chambersburg you can stop and visit the Franklin County Restored Jail, a pink brick building which now houses the Kittochtinny Historical Society library and museum. Built in 1818, the jail survived the 1863 burning of Chambersburg by the Confederate Army; it is now open to the public. Also in the Chambersburg area is the former site of private Fort Benjamin Chambers, circa 1755. Marked by a boulder at the rear of Chambersburg's Rosedale parking lot, the defunct fort was erected by this enterprising settler to protect his home and grist mill from Indian attack. Conococheague Creek, which ran between mill and house, provided the water that powered the mill.

Following the Frontier Trail signs, bear north from Chambersburg, leaving Route 30. Just south of the Letterkenny Army Depot, you'll find Rock Spring Church, a lovely colonial church built in 1794 by Scotch-Irish Presbyterians. Of note are the handmade leaded windows, brick floors, wooden pews, and especially its glaring lack of chimneys, designed to resist Indian attacks. Since it lies within what is now army depot land, the church has been preserved by concerned citizens. It is open to the public during the summer through the Franklin County church tours. For more information, write to Franklin County Tourist Council, 75 South Second Street, Chambersburg, Pennsylvania 17201.

Continuing westward to Edenville, you'll pass two historic markers. The first indicates the 1756 site of another private fort, Fort McCord. Here local white settlers were killed by Indians and their fort burned to the ground. The second marker commemorates Mary Jamison, the "white squaw." Near this marker, the 15-year-old girl, her family, and a neighboring family were captured by the Indians. All were killed except Mary—who later married an Indian—and one boy.

Returning to Route 30, you will pass Fort Loudon, intended by settlers as protection from the Indians but used to hold some of them captive as criminals against the British crown. The first blood of the American Revolution was spilled at this site in 1764, 10 years before the start of the Revolutionary War in New England. The fort is being restored and will be opened to the public in the near future.

Follow the Frontier Trail markers south of Cove Gap, near the county line in order to visit the James Buchanan birthplace and park.

At this point you must decide whether to continue westward on Route 30 or to complete the loop of Frontier Trail. If you have time, turn east onto Route 16, where Frontier Trail markers will lead you to Anderson's Mill (circa 1848) and Martin's Mill covered bridge, which spans the Conococheague Creek to connect Antrim and Montgomery townships. In the Greencastle-Kauffman area, you'll pass a monument that notes the Enoch Brown School Massacre of 1764. Another monument commemorates Corporal Rihl who, in 1863, was the first Union soldier to be killed north of the Mason-Dixon line.

Heading east to the Waynesboro area, you'll find Welty's Scottish-style bridge, a near-miracle of engineering that has survived two centuries with almost no repairs. There's also Renfrew Park and Museum, an 1815 stone farmhouse full of Pennsylvania folk art. It's open March through mid-December, by appointment only [call (717) 762-4723]. From there, visit the eighteenth-century John Bourns House and the Emmanuel Chapel, where in 1858 John Brown taught for several months while he planned his famous attack on Harpers Ferry.

If you take the time to drive the southern leg of the Frontier Trail loop, you can retrace your treads westward on Route 30. If not, you can return to Route 30 via Route 16 west, traveling through scenic Fulton County from McConnellsburg to Breezewood.

Next comes Bedford County, and just west of Breezewood, you'll reach Juniata Crossings over the Raystown Branch of the Juniata River. Before you reach Bedford, visit the Lutz Historical Museum, between Route 30 and the Pennsylvania Turnpike.

The town of Bedford is difficult to resist; scores of attractions tempt you to stop and stretch your legs. Most of the charming historic buildings were built during the mid-1800s, but several date back to the eighteenth century, including a 1770 building that served as President Washington's headquarters during the 1794 Whiskey Rebellion and is today a national landmark. If you have extra time to pause here, take all or part of the walking tour through Bedford (see *Country Roads,* page 153).

Before you leave, you might want to compare today's Bedford with Old Bedford Village, a colonial village reconstructed of authentic buildings of the age gathered from the surrounding countryside. Launched in a bicentennial gesture on July 4, 1976, the village is open year-round and features demonstrations at the working farm, in addition to quilting, spinning, and smithy demonstrations. Authentic structures in the village include a covered bridge and an eight-sided schoolhouse said to have been built by the Quakers to prevent the devil from cornering their children. About two miles west, north of Route 30 on Pennsyl Hollow Road, you can visit the Algonkin Gap Indian Relic Museum, whose displays were collected in Bedford County. At the intersection of Route 30 and Route 31 is the Old Forks Inn, built in 1764 and known to the pioneer travelers who stopped there as Bonnet's Tavern. If you'd like a real visual treat, take a side trip south on Route 31 and over the 10-mile Old Glade Pike known as the Little Skyline Drive.

Toward Schellsburg, drivers have the option of stopping at several historic and recreational sites. First you'll pass the Sleepy Hollow Tavern, built in 1775. In the Schellsburg area, Union Church, circa 1806, warrants a look inside. This rustic log church also has a cemetery that will tantalize headstone readers. Stop at Shawnee State Park and Lake (south of Route 30), or take the kids to Storyland (north of Route 30).

At the Bedford-Somerset County line, you enter ski country. Peaks in the area reach almost 3,000 feet; the wild streams make this territory beautiful year-round. In the Laurel Hill and Chestnut Ridge Mountain area the first ski area you'll reach is Laurel Mountain, which is directly off Route 30 on the Somerset-Westmoreland County line. Less than 10 miles west, near Ligonier, is the Sugarbush Mountain Ski Area, south of Route 30. For the kids, Story Book Forest is north of Route 30 in the same area.

After the ski slopes, you begin to see the signs of metropolitan Pittsburgh so, unless you like Pittsburgh, end your Route 30 trip at Greensburg.

Country roads

Covered bridges tour: about 50 miles through Bedford County. County.

Jam-packed with historic sites and other tourist attractions, Bedford County also boasts an impressive list of covered bridges. It once sported 74 of them—more than any other county in the state—but now has only 15, and preservationists fear that some of these are fated for the wrecking ball.

Many of the covered bridges left standing in Pennsylvania have survived through the efforts of local citizens, and I hope these relics of Mid-Atlantic history will continue to survive. The sites are quite popular with photographers. The tour described below gives you a chance to compare the styles and sizes of the bridges built during pioneer days.

While many of the bridges are on or near main routes, some of them are on back roads in small villages. If you don't have the time or the desire to take in all 15 bridges, choose one section of the tour—several locations offer two or three within a small area—and stop for a quick cruise through these if time is limited.

The best place to begin this tour is at Route 30 near Breezewood. About one mile west of Breezewood and south of the Pennsylvania Turnpike, you'll find a group of three bridges over Brush Creek. The Jackson Bridge, 97 feet long, is three miles south of Breezewood on Route 412. McDaniel Bridge, in East Providence Township, on Route 419, is 116 feet long. The third bridge in the area is Felton Mills on Route 05021; this one is 100 feet long.

Return to Route 30 west and turn north on Route 26. Proceed to Yellow Creek (about 10 miles). Hall's Mill Bridge—95 feet long—crosses Yellow Creek on Route 528. From there, take Routes 868 and 869 west to Osterburg. At Osterburg, take Route 220 south to the junction with Route 56 and turn north west to Route 56. Two bridges are in the Osterburg-Pleasantville area. The first, Bowser, is 97 feet of covered bridge over Bob's Creek. Near Osterburg, it can be reached from Route 575. Just east of Pleasantville, you'll find Snooks Bridge. Snooks Bridge is on Route 578; half a mile from Route 56, it's 80 feet long.

At Pleasantville, take Route 96 south. There are three bridges between Pleasantville and Schellsburg. The first is on Route 559 near Ryot, half a mile east of Route 96. It is 81 feet long, and it runs over Dunnings Creek. New Paris Bridge is just east of that town on Route 96. It crosses Shawnee Creek and is 71 feet long. Knisely Bridge, 79 feet long, crosses Dunnings Creek. It can be reached from Leg. Route 05098, a thousand feet south of Route 56.

Continue southward on Route 96. You'll find two bridges in the Schellsburg area. The first is on Route 443, southwest of the town, just off Route 30. The 71-foot Colvin Bridge crosses Shawnee Creek. Palo Alto Bridge is in Londonderry Township on Leg. Route 05007. Just south of Hyndman, the bridge can be seen from Route 96 if you have trouble finding it.

Drive to Route 31 and turn off onto Route 418, west of Manns Choice. Turner's Bridge, 86 feet long, is over the Rays-town Branch of the Juniata River.

Finally, you can return to Route 30, heading east, and visit Old Bedford Village off Route 200. One of the restored village's authentic buildings is Claycomb covered bridge, transplanted to the village in 1976. It's also the longest of the county's covered bridges—126 feet.

If you are willing to go out of your way or if you are traveling into Maryland, you can visit Hewitt Bridge. The 86-foot bridge is in Southampton Township on Route 305. Just a mile north of the state line, the bridge crosses Town Creek.

Covered bridges, while they are disappearing, can be found throughout most of Pennsylvania, and in many other areas in the Mid-Atlantic (see *Country roads* in other regions of Pennsylvania and in other Mid-Atlantic states).

Driving deep into the past: about 25 miles through York County.

The high point of this tour is in driving over *real* back roads to an authentic iron furnace and the woodland corners of a scenic county. The tour starts in the town of York. Although this town has lost most of its Colonial look, its preservation efforts have brought some good results. Besides some well preserved historic sites, there are produce stands stocked by the local farms.

Start the trip at 1455 Mount Zion Road, at the Tourist Bureau's Information Center, which will supply you with directions. maps and other literature about the region. Leave the parking lot from the rear, turning right on Mount Zion Road. In about a mile start looking for a church that sits on the hill; just over the top of the hill, turn right on a hidden road that leads to Rocky Ridge County Park. Drive through and leave the park by turning right on Mount Zion Road. Drive about a mile to North Sherman Street and turn left. Then take the first road on the right, Mundis Mill Road.

The York House,
a historic site
in the town of York.
*(Photo courtesy of
Colonial York County)*

In addition to some carefully restored historic sites, the city of York has an interesting central market full of produce grown in the area.
(*Photo courtesy of Colonial York County*)

York County's Log House.
(*Photo courtesy of Colonial York County*)

After about half a mile, you'll go over the Codorus Creek Bridge. Note the pretty farm on your right. Drive another half a mile and turn right on Locust Lane. This is another hidden turn-off, so look for the burned barn on your right past the bridge. The road then covers a scenic stretch, following the course of the creek for about one-and-a-half miles to Mundis Mills. Between Locust and the town of Mundis Mills, turn right on Mundis Race Road near the yellow barn, drive half a mile to the entrance of John Rudy County Park and then another half a mile through the park.

Old Codorus Furnace is located at the end of a backwoods drive in York County. *(Photo by David Adams)*

At Mundis Mills the road rejoins North Sherman Road. Turn left and drive about two miles to the marker for Old Codorus Furnace. Turn right at the marker and drive a little more than two miles to the furnace. Also called Hallam Forge, Codorus Furnace produced pig iron that was turned into supplies for both the Revolutionary War and the War of 1812. Operating between 1765 and 1850, the forge was rebuilt in 1948; you can picnic right next to it.

From the furnace, the road runs uphill through four miles of forest filled with wildlife, possibly the most scenic stretch of this tour. On the other side of the woods drive through the town of Fairmont. Continue another half-mile and turn right on Accomac Road. Drive about one-and-a-half miles and turn right just before the Route 30 underpass. The road is called Horn Road; you'll find an old stone house on its corner.

In about a mile, Chimney Rock Road enters from the right. Keep driving straight on, turning left in about half a mile on Tracey School Road. Drive half a mile to Route 30 and make another right turn. Drive two-and-a-half miles on Route 30 to the Mount Zion Road exit. Turn right off the exit to return to the Information Center (half a mile).

NORTHWESTERN PENNSYLVANIA (Great Lakes Gateway)

Scenic drives and country roads

Northwestern lake country tour: about 100 miles of connected country roads through Crawford County. From Pymatuning to Canadohta—driving the Appalachian Plateau among some of the largest natural lakes in Pennsylvania.

Northwestern Pennsylvania is known for its huge reservoir where the ducks walk on the fish. Yes, that's right. At the spillway on Pymatuning Reservoir, you can watch the local waterfowl casually hopping from fish to fish. If Crawford County takes a back seat to its eastern neighbors in terms of forest lands, it makes up for that lack in its glory of natural lakes. This tour takes you crisscrossing over the plateau from lake to lake. Much of the route involves backtracking to take in all the sights, so you can break the whole into its individual country roads for shorter tours.

The eastern part of the county is hilly and rugged. The west, on the Ohio border, gives way to gentle slopes, shallow streams, and fertile valleys where dairy farms thrive. Start at Pymatuning Reservoir, which crosses the Ohio-Pennsylvania border, and head for the causeway off Route 285. You'll cross a two-mile stretch of the lake and take Route 285 east. Turn left on Leg. Route 20003, and another left on Leg. Route 20006, which crosses the lake. On the right is the famous spillway, where the ducks walk on the piles of fish. You can stop and feed bread to the members of this crazy water show or proceed a little farther north to .Ford Island. Operated by the Pennsylvania Game Commission, this island offers picnic areas and a Wildwater Fowl Museum. There's a viewer that allows you to zoom in on an eagle's nest and lots of other wildlife to observe.

On the other side of the lake, near Linesville, you'll find the Pennsylvania Fish Commission Hatchery. If you're interested, it is one of the largest hatcheries in the world; it even has an albino trout. Turn left at Linesville to Ferris Park for picnics, swimming, or rather primitive camping. Turn around and head back through Linesville; turn left on Route 618, just west of Conneaut Lake. There you'll find a country store and an Indian museum in an old log house moved from Butler County. It has authentic 1800s furnishings and offers the usual farm-craft demonstrations.

Drive north on Route 618 to two amusement areas especially good for families. Conneaut Lake Park boasts that its rides offer 217 ways to have fun, and nearby Fairyland Forest has a Mother Goose theme for the toddler set.

For a scenic detour, take Route 18 south from the north end of Conneaut Lake. This is the largest natural lake in the state, and one of seven major recreational lakes in the county. Drive to Meadville, pass Allegheny College, and take Route 86 north to Woodcock Dam on the lake by the same name. A new park, Colonial Crawford, is being developed there.

Continue north to Cambridge Springs, a tourist mecca from

The Wild Waterfowl Museum near Pymatuning Lake.
(Photo courtesy of Crawford County Tourist Association)

On the north banks of Pymatuning Lake, this Pennsylvania Fish Commission Hatchery is one of the largest in the world.
(Photo courtesy of Crawford County Tourist Association)

(Above) Snowmobile races are part of Conneaut Lake's annual Snow-Ball Festival.
(Below) From Conneaut Lake Park you can visit Fairyland Forest, a children's paradise in Pennsylvania.
(Photo courtesy of Crawford County Tourist Association)

The Spring House at Riverside Inn in Cambridge Springs, where visitors have drunk the allegedly curative waters since colonial days.
(Photo courtesy of Crawford County Tourist Association)

the late 1800s to the early 1900s. You can partake of the spring waters by walking the boardwalk to The Spring House from the town. Unfortunately, in 1977 part of the boardwalk was damaged, blocking the path.

North of Cambridge Springs is an area that is truly beautiful in the fall. The surrounding mountains offer Mount Pleasant Ski Resort. Backtrack on Route 86 to Woodcock and turn left on Leg. Route 20070. Drive southeast to Route 77, where you can stop at Bechtel's sugar museum and the Pioneer Village. Craft demonstrations are given on some weekends, and you can see the early nineteenth-century loghouse. But the highlight is being able to taste the sweet maple sugars, syrups, and candies.

Turn onto Route 77 east and watch for the remains of John Brown's tannery on your right. The abolitionist lived there for 10 years, using the tannery as a stop on the Underground Railroad. Continuing on Route 77, turn left on Leg. Route 20083 and right on Leg. Route 20084 to Canadohta Lake, another water recreation spot.

Returning to Route 77, turn right (south) on Route 8 to Titusville. The main attraction there is the Drake Well Museum, commemorating the spot where oil was discovered in 1859. The intriguing thing on the site is a ghost town, Pithole, which had 10,000 residents during the 1860s oil boom.

South of Titusville, on Route 8, you'll pass Carter's Pheasant Farm. Take Route 27 west from Titusville to Meadville, passing the Frosty Ski Slopes and the road to Erie National Wildlife Refuge. To reach this 5,000-acre refuge, turn left on Route 173, and drive about two miles south of Mt. Hope. The waterfowl are abundant in the park.

Continuing west, turn left on Thurston Road just outside of Meadville. Turn left on the Alden Street Extension and right at the sign for Tamarack Lake (Leg. Route 20033). Drive around the lake to Leg. Route 20032, and take Township Route 578 back to Meadville.

Canadohta Lake, Crawford County, is one of seven large watering holes that attract vacationers to northwestern Pennsylvania.
(Photo courtesy of Crawford County Tourist Association)

Northwestern Pennsylvania played a major role in the launching of the American oil industry. In Crawford County you can visit the oil museum and this replica of the Drake Oil Well, with derrick and engine house.

SOUTHWEST PENNSYLVANIA (The Laurel Highlands)

The natural terrain of southwestern Pennsylvania is disrupted by metropolitan Pittsburgh, limiting the truly scenic routes in this region to the Laurel Highlands of Fayette and Somerset counties. Many scenic drives and country roads, especially those leading to historic areas, are available to drivers, but the population in this part of Pennsylvania is a little denser than in the central farmlands or the northern forest and mountains. If you have taken the Pennsylvania Turnpike west across the state, you'll remember that the mountains fold into foothills outside of Pittsburgh, finally giving way to the plains in eastern Ohio.

Scenic drives

The most obvious scenic and historic route through this territory is Route 40, the National Pike. For details on that tour, see

Chapter 6. You can also check details on the western leg of the Route 30 tour (see *Scenic drives, Southern Pennsylvania*). And, for a city-side scenic tour, try the Ohio River route running west of Pittsburgh (*Scenic drives,* Chapter 7).

The Laurel Highlands offer some of the highest peaks in the state, and the entire area is a vacation center. Again, many routes are scenic. The ones described below are chosen for their views and unusual points of interest. For good examples of this territory's flavor, try driving Route 271 from Ligonier, east to Johnstown. It's about a 20-mile tour through Westmoreland and Cambria counties, offering stops at Fort Ligonier and a side trip to the Church in the Wilderness to the north. Laurel Hill and its surrounding peaks rise to 2,800 feet in height.

Another nice tour is Route 653 from Normalville east to New Centerville, followed by Route 281 northeast to Somerset (see *Country roads* off Route 281, page). This 25-mile drive can be a continuation of scenic drive Route 381 (page), crossing Laurel Hill and Laurel Hill Creek, plus the ski areas of Fayette and Somerset counties. The following drive is one of the most spectacular, presenting some of the most diverse points of interest. Because of its appeal, you won't be entirely alone, but the company of a few fellow sightseers shouldn't lessen your enjoyment.

Route 381:   about 15 miles through Fayette County. From Fort Necessity to Normalville—a perfect mountain drive through the Laurel Highlands.

Since this tour is only 15 miles long, it can be completed in a short time, but if you stop at every possible attraction, it could take a full day or more. Start at Fort Necessity National Battlefield, just south of Route 40 and west of Route 381. This is a touristy spot, so if you don't mind missing it, take Route 381 ngth past Braddock's Grave (another touristy spot) about five miles to Ohiopyle Falls, a beautiful state park. To reach the park, follow the signs from Ohiopyle Borough or enter at the Cucumber Falls end by driving three-tenths of a mile south of Ohiopyle on Route 381 and turning right on Leg. Route 26071.

Cucumber Falls is one-fifth of a mile from there. With 18,000 acres, this is the state's largest state park. The wild Youghiogheny River runs 14 miles through the park; the two falls are gorgeous; and you can take a nature trail to Ferncliff Peninsula, a 100-acre peninsula formed by a sharp horseshoe curve in the river.

Drive five miles north to Fallingwater. This 1936 Frank Lloyd Wright house is on the left side of the road on the southern edge of Mill Run. One of the architect's most famous designs, the house is built over a waterfall on Bear Run.

Just a half mile north of the house is Bear Run Nature Preserve—3,500 acres of forests, trails, and the courses of Bear Run and Laurel Run.

From the preserve, drive five miles north to Normalville, where you can end your trip, or proceed east on Route 653 for extra scenic jaunts.

Country roads

Two covered bridge tours: various distances through Somerset County.

The principal remnants of rural colonial Pennsylvania in the Laurel Highlands are covered bridges and iron furnaces. Other historic sites abound, including houses and churches, battlefields and log cabins. The following tours are jaunts among several of the covered bridges that have survived in Somerset County.

Route 281   (south of Somerset)

Between New Lexington and Ursina, on a north-south line, you'll find three covered bridges that are easily reached from Route 281. Starting in Somerset, take Route 281 south to Leg. Route 55040, west of New Lexington. The road runs over Laurel Creek on the old "Clay Pike," and leads to King's Bridge.

The second bridge, located in the town of Barronvale, south of Route 653, is called Barronvale Bridge. The third bridge is near Humbert. Take Route 281 south from Somerset until you reach the "T" in the road a mile outside of Ursina. Turn north along Laurel Hill Stream there and drive about a mile north toward Humbert. There you'll find Lower Humbert Bridge.

Route 281   (north of Somerset)

Starting again in Somerset, take Route 281 north to U.S. Route 30 and drive north on Route 403 to Tire Hill. The first covered bridge on this tour—Shaffer Bridge—is about 25 miles north of Somerset, east of Route 403 and northwest of Tire Hill. You should be able to see it from Route 403.

To reach the second bridge, take route 281 north (actually east) from Somerset to Route 30 and drive to Stoystown. Drive one-half mile east and turn right on the first road you pass. This will lead you to the Trostletown Bridge. The whole trip is about 10 miles long.

The final bridge on the tour—Glessner Bridge—can be reached by taking Route 31 east from Somerset to White Reservoir on the ridge about three miles east. Drive another few miles over a flat section of road and turn left to Shanksville on Leg. Route 55068. Drive north about a mile and turn left on the dirt road to Glessner Bridge.

6

Beyond Concrete— Interstate Drives with a Difference

The truly scenic route

Interstate highways cut across the Mid-Atlantic states in all directions, and most travelers tend to limit their long-distance drives to these superefficient multilane roads. Considering the aim of this book, however, I'd like to suggest a few truly scenic, continuous routes to carry you from state to state. Back roads can always be connected, of course, and in this densely populated region of the nation there's no such thing as "You can't get there from here."

The drives following geographically natural routes are probably the best for interstate travel. For instance, you can create an Ocean Drive Unlimited by taking New Jersey's Ocean Drive to Cape May Point, and taking the ferry to Lewes, Delaware. From Lewes, you can continue down the Atlantic coast, passing Rehoboth Beach and crossing into Maryland at Ocean City. (For details on each leg of this extended trip, see *Scenic drives* in each state.)

167

This Ocean City boardwalk is one of many along the New Jersey, Delaware, and Maryland seashore towns.
(This and all photographs in this chapter courtesy of Maryland Office of Tourist Development)

Some of the U.S. highways described in part in previous chapters may be extended to cross state lines. Keep in mind, however, that the sections described were chosen for their scenic attributes; if you extend your trip, you may encounter less enticing surroundings. And, of course, any extended trip on a secondary highway will add to your total driving time.

U.S. Route 30 may be extended eastward through Pennsylvania, still scenic for a good stretch, and on into New Jersey to Atlantic City. Chester County's (Pennsylvania) U.S. Route 322 can be extended to the east and to the west. This old highway connects Erie, Pennsylvania, and Atlantic City. Route 209, the Pennsylvania-side Delaware Water Gap tour, can be taken north into New York, from Port Jervis through the Catskills, ending at Kingston. Or you may continue through Pennsylvania on Route 20, ending on the east bank of the Susquehanna River, north of Harrisburg. From there you can hook up with the Susquehanna River Tour (see *Scenic drives, Central Pennsylvunia*).

Perhaps the only real "un-interstate" in the Mid-Atlantic states is U.S. Route 40, the old National Pike.

National Pike-plus: about 340 miles through Ohio County (West Virginia); Washington, Fayette, and Somerset counties (Pennsylvania); Garrett, Allegheny, Washington, Frederick, Howard, Baltimore, Harford, and Cecil counties (Maryland); and New Castle County (Delaware). From Wheeling to Wilmington—driving America's first interstate, one of the most scenic drives through the Mid-Atlantic states.

This tour is a perfect introduction to the Mid-Atlantic states if you're unfamiliar with the area. It is a good scenic route for travelers heading east from the Midwest, as well as an alternate to U.S. Routes 70 and 79, and the Pennsylvania Turnpike (Route 76). Starting from Ohio, you drive right into the mountains of West Virginia and Pennsylvania, a welcome relief from the flatlands of the Midwest. The old National Road winds up, down, and around mountains, through narrow gaps and, for vacationers with extra time on their hands, along scores of historic towns. To appreciate a Route 40 drive to its fullest, you must understand the history of the road, the towns it fostered, the people who traveled it, and how it fared in a match-up against the transportation modes introduced by the industrial revolution.

The National Road Bill, 1806, called for the construction of a route connecting the Ohio River with the navigable waters emptying into the Atlantic Ocean. According to the original plan, the road would run from Cumberland, Maryland, on the Potomac, to Steubenville, Ohio. But the project ran into snags when the states involved refused their cooperation unless the road detoured to Uniontown and Washington, Pennsylvania, as well as Wheeling, West Virginia. Construction of this stone superhighway was thus delayed for five years while the states argued for their respective interests. It wasn't until 1813 that the first 103 miles were completed.

Their completion brought a boom of jobs for settlers along the road's course. It brought travelers of all kinds, in their prairie schooners and stagecoaches. It was used by the Pony Express, by cattlemen, and by packs of peddlers. Unhappily, it also brought the highwaymen—road thieves who hid out in places like the evergreen forest over Mt. Savage, just west of Cumberland. Travelers who made it through this spooky woodland unscathed considered themselves lucky and plowed down the road to stop at one of the road's many inns and taverns. The traffic was fast and heavy on this route. Some of the towns and taverns erected around it can be seen today.

A mere three years after the National Pike reached Indianapolis, the Baltimore and Ohio Railroad tracks reached Wheeling, and for the next 25 years traffic on the road dwindled. The federal government eventually turned the road over to the states that it crossed, and for a time Route 40 was a toll road. Some of the attractive tollgate houses still stand alongside the road. It was not until the invention of the auto that the road came into its own again. At that time, Route 40 was pushed westward to Vandalia, Illinois.

Other relics of the past available to sightseers include covered and stone bridges, old iron furnaces, mountain passages first blazed by Indians, and some almost-untouched wilderness. The condition of the road varies. Its height and curves can make it hazardous in snow, and in some areas the road is in serious need of repair.

On the western half of the trip, be sure to follow the signs for *scenic* Route 40. A new superhighway, Route 40-48, runs generally parallel to the old National Pike and offers higher speed and better road conditions. Route 70, which also runs parallel to the pike, is—in many stretches—the same road.

Enter Route 40 at Wheeling in northwestern West Virginia. If you're traveling the interstates, you can reach Route 40 via Route 70. Drive through rolling mountains about 30 miles from Wheeling to Washington, Pennsylvania. Just west of Washington, look for an unusual S-curve bridge.

In Washington, the road jogs southeast toward Uniontown and Cumberland. About 12 miles east of Washington, you'll reach the Scenery Hill, where the Century Inn is located. The oldest tavern in continuous use on the National Pike, it opened its doors in 1794. Today it is open to the public from Good Friday through December 15.

Drive about 12 miles and cross the pretty Monongahela River

near the Washington-Fayette County line. On the east side of the river is Brownsville. On Front Street you can explore Nemacolin Castle, named for a famous Indian scout who helped blaze the westward trail. During the 1790s, Brownsville was known as the "river gateway to the west." Nemacolin Castle was built around a 1759 structure, old Fort Burd, which was a trading post, refuge, and travel rest of 22 rooms.

Four miles west of Uniontown you'll pass the restored Searights Tollhouse. One of two remaining on the Pennsylvania section of the pike, this brick building was the toll collector's living quarters. Tolls were in effect until 1905, paid by *everyone*—pedestrians and animals as well as persons in vehicles—with the exception of churchgoers.

In Uniontown, U.S. Route 40 becomes Main Street, and it runs by a notable old county courthouse. For a scenic side trip, take Township Road 688 south from Route 40 to Lick Hollow State Forest. Five or six miles east of Uniontown is Point Lookout, which offers a beautiful view of the valley below from Mt. Summit on Chestnut Ridge's western slope. Atop Mt. Summit is Mt. Summit Inn, one of the area's lovely resorts. Five miles south are the famous Laurel Caverns, the largest natural caves in North America north of the Mason-Dixon line.

Next you'll pass Hopwood, a popular stop for pike travelers with many old buildings remaining. Detour on Hopwood Fairchance Road for a look at the 60-foot white cliffs that inspired a local legend. In 1810, Polly Williams supposedly was thrown to her death from the cliffs by an unfaithful lover.

West of Route 381 (11 miles east of Uniontown) you can stop at Fort Necessity National Battlefield, where 22-year-old George Washington engaged in his first battle, also the first battle of the French and Indian War. Just west of the entrance to the battlefield is Mount Washington Tavern Museum, an old stagecoach stop built between 1824 and 1828. In the distance you can see the 60-foot Jumonville Cross, which lights up at night. (For a beautiful side trip on Route 381, see *Scenic drives, Southwestern Pennsylvania*.)

At Farmington on Route 381, you'll find the Nemacolin Trail Hunting Reserve and Animal Farm, with facilities for camping, hunting and fishing, and overnight accommodations. About 10 miles east is Youghiogheny River Lake. This well-known canoeing river was dammed for flood control, creating a 2,840-acre lake near the county line, surrounded by farms. On the other side of the lake is Addison, where you'll see the other remaining Pennsylvania tollhouse. About five or ten miles northeast of Addison you might be able to see Mt. Davis, the highest point in Pennsylvania—3,213 feet.

Cross into Maryland's Garrett County to the town of Keysers Ridge. The first thing of note on the Maryland side is Savage River State Forest—the largest in the state. It has 53,000 acres of near-wilderness. The wealth of trees that surround you include wild cherry, sugar and red maples, yellow and black birches, beech, basswood, white pine, hemlock, tulip poplar, and hickory.

About five miles east, one mile west of Grantsville, you will pass the Fuller-Baker Log House. Built some time after 1813, it is said to be typical of the Allegheny frontier homes but larger, thought possibly to have been a tavern.

In Grantsville, Route 40 is Main Street; the town grew up around the pike. There is famous Casselman Hotel, built in the early 1800s and opened in 1824. One of its current attractions is its exceptional country-cured hams, served in the dining room.

Casselman Bridge can be seen from the old National Pike, U.S. Route 40.

Artisans abound in the charming town of Penn Alps in Garrett County.

One mile east of town is Casselman Bridge, north of the bridge that you cross today. When it was built in 1813, it was the longest single-span stone arch bridge in the world. Today it is a National Historic Landmark, with a five-acre roadside state park for picnics.

To the east, you'll find Penn Alps, a delightful town with a Mennonite restaurant and craft center in an 1820 log house. In the town are more than 900 artisans working at native handcrafts. Nearby is Stanton's Mill. Built in 1797, it is the oldest Garrett County grist mill and is still going strong. Four miles east of Grantsville is one of the oldest road inns built on the pike. The Stone House, formerly Tomlinson Inn, lies on the western edge of Little Meadows Valley and was built in 1818. On the north side of Route 40 is the access to Braddock Trail.

Now running through private as well as public lands, the trail is being replotted for use as a walking trail.

About 10 miles east of Grantsville is Frostburg, another National Road town, which sits in the shadow of 2,850-foot Savage Mountain. Five miles east of Cumberland at the intersection of the National Road and Route 55 is Clarysville Bridge. One of the first bridges built on the National Road, the stone arch bridge is the last of its kind standing in Allegheny County. Next door is the 1807 Clarysville Inn. About one mile east, just west of Route 53, is the quaint LaVale Toll Gate House. Built in 1836, it was used during the period when Maryland charged tolls on the road. in the period of 1835 to 1878.

This well-preserved remnant of the National Pike's golden days is the LaVale Toll Gate House, just west of Cumberland along U.S Route 40.

Next you'll reach one of the most scenic stretches of the National Road. Just west of Cumberland, the road runs through The Narrows. This treacherous path through the mountains was wisely bypassed on most of the earlier westward trails and is today bypassed by Route 48, so be sure to stay on Route 40 to see it. When you reach historic Cumberland, you can stop for an hour or a day to explore the historic sites.

Two miles east of Cumberland, you'll pass Colonial Manor. Built in the mid-nineteenth century as a tavern and later used as an 1864 Civil War hospital, the brick inn has interesting interior woodwork.

Between Cumberland and Hancock there are no stops of special interest. Halfway through the 30 miles between those cities, scenic Route 40 branches north and runs through Green Ridge State Forest. There you're bound to see wild turkey, grouse, squirrel, and deer, all set against a verdant backdrop. About eight miles east of Cumberland is a scenic overlook, and when you reach Hancock, you can visit the Chesapeake and Ohio Canal Museum.

Continue eastward, being sure to stay with Route 40 when it splits with Route 70 at Indian Springs. About five miles west of Hagerstown, watch for the old Conococheague bridge. Situated about 200 feet north of the new bridge's west end, the five-arch stone span bridge was built in 1819.

Like Cumberland, Hagerstown offers many historic sites. You can spend as much time there as you like. From the town, take Alternate Route 40 (Route 40A) southeast rather than Route 40. About two miles southwest of Hagerstown, this detour takes you to eighteenth-century Funkstown with its quaint shops and intriguing architecture.

Drive about 10 miles to Washington Monument State Park near Boonsboro. On its 100 acres are the first monument erected to George Washington (in 1827, on South Mountain), the 1730 Old South Mountain Inn, and a section of the Appalachian Trail . . . to say nothing of the views.

Drive about 15 miles to Frederick, where Routes 40 and 70 rejoin and run together to Baltimore. Between Frederick and Ellicott City, about 35 miles, the scenery is less distinctive, but you still have a choice of historic sites. On Ellicott City's Maryland Avenue is the first terminus of America's first railroad, the famed B & O. From Ellicott City, drive through or around Baltimore. (For details on Baltimore city roads, see Chapter 7.)

Between the eastern outskirts of Baltimore and Wilmington, Delaware, the mountains finally give way to rolling farmland. The sights and attractions are fewer, but several state parks and forests are along the way. In Abington, about 15 miles east of Baltimore, is St. Mary's Episcopal Church. Located at 2501 Emmorton Road, this 1848 church has the only complete set of William Butterfield glass windows in the country.

Your next stop should be at Havre de Grave, about 13 miles east. The Susquehanna River runs nearby, and at the end of Lafayette Street is the 1829 Concord Point Lighthouse. On the banks of the Susquehanna and the Tidewater Canal is an 1840 Lock House with a museum.

Cross the river and jog momentarily off Route 40 to Route 7. Drive a couple of miles to Principio Furnace, the site of the first ironworks in the British colonies. There cannon and ammunition for the Revolutionary armies were made; the furnace continued to operate until 1900. Consider taking a detour off Route 7 to Elk Neck State Forest, 3,000 acres with a tranquil pond, wildlife food plots, and an exceptional population of white-tailed deer.

From the forest return to Route 40 and cross the Maryland-Delaware line. From there, it's about 20 miles northeast to Wilmington, where you can stop or go on to parts north.

Stop at Concord Point Lighthouse at Havre de Grace, Harford County, for a bayside view.

7

Hidden Treasures—Country Roads in the Cities

THE WILDS OF THE MID-ATLANTIC

If you have not yet explored the wilds of the Mid-Atlantic region, you may firmly believe there is no such thing. Granted, the eastern seaboard between Boston and Richmond has been described as one huge unbroken megalopolis. And, true, the most densely populated plots of land in the country are found right here in the heart of the Mid-Atlantic area. But if you have even skimmed the preceding chapters and you still don't believe there's solitude and scenery here for the auto driver, I can say no more.

If you want wide open spaces in a really big way, go west. If you're looking for a guarantee that you won't see another vehicle on the road throughout your trip, take a walk (somewhere else). The following trips are meant to lead you to the hidden, or otherwise noteworthy, corners of the huge Eastern cities. As such, they can be considered scenic drives or country roads only in relation to their surroundings. Should you decide to read on, keep in mind that one person's alley is another person's country road. If nothing else, the following suggestions should give city scorners a look at the natural beauty still available in the urban areas.

New York City

It is really difficult to find an isolated spot in the Big Apple (but it can be done). For deserted routes, your best bet is to try the Long Island beaches or any other summer locales during the winter. The tours listed below are short drives, meant to include the best views of a natural world that seems totally obscured by its manmade structures.

West Battery tour

This tour, taking in the original battery and the Statue of Liberty, certainly doesn't offer solitude, but if you haven't seen these landmarks, they are worth a trip.

To reach Battery Park, take the Brooklyn Bridge north or FDR Drive south to the tip of Manhattan Island . There you'll see Castle Clinton, the original battery. Built in 1811, this structure was one of four forts built in New York City, although this fort saw no action during the ensuing War of 1812. After the war, the building became Castle Garden, a huge public arena. To increase its worth as a theater, a roof was added in the 1840s, and there Jenny Lind made her 1850 American debut. By 1855 the castle had changed hands again and had begun welcoming immigrants from Europe. In 1896 the structure was turned into the New York City Aquarium. When the aquarium was moved in 1941, the castle was destined for the wrecking ball. But concerned citizens sounded the alarm, and the National Park Service eventually took over the battery. Coincidentally, the overanxious wrecking crew had already demolished the roof and other 1840s additions, leaving the battery with its original 1811 appearance. Reopened in 1975, the battery now holds fairs, concerts, and other events, and New Yorkers can picnic on its pretty grounds.

From Battery Park, you can take the Circle Line's Statue of Liberty Ferry. Make the climb to the top of the Statue, or explore the American Museum of Immigration on the island. You can see all of the New York area from the statue, including nearby Ellis Island, the most famous of the immigrant landing depots.

Gateway National Recreation Area

A multisectioned park still under development, Gateway is intended to preserve the natural beauty left along the New York and New Jersey bays and the Atlantic Ocean. The most interesting divisions are Staten Island and the Jamaica Bay Unit.

To reach Staten Island, take the famous ferry or drive across the Verrazzano Narrows Bridge. From New Jersey, you can cross the Bayonne Bridge or the Outerbridge from Perth Amboy. From the Verrazzano Narrows Bridge, take Seaside Boulevard to Midland Avenue and drive south on Hyland Boulevard a few miles to Great Kills Park. Pheasant abound in the park, and you'll have another vantage point from which to view this busy port. For an extended tour of the island, drive around the residential areas—some of the homes are beautiful.

The Jamacia Bay Unit features Jamaica Bay Wildlife Refuge, a cluster of diverse islands in this huge bay. The refuge is located on the Atlantic Flyway. You can see more than 300 species of shore birds and waterfowl as they stop here on their migration route. From Shore Parkway to Rockaway Freeway Beach Channel Drive, you can drive the six miles of Cross Bay Boulevard through the refuge. At the Cross Bay (toll) Bridge, you can drive west to the two other subdivisions of the Jamaica Bay Unit—Riis Park and Breezy Point.

City Island

City Island is a slightly different type of island not far from LaGuardia Airport. East of the Bronx and Mount Vernon, it's a pleasant side trip from any part of New York and has one of the best seafood restaurants around—Thwaite's. Be sure to stop for some of their unique clam chowder, which is a mixture of the New England and Manhattan styles.

To reach the island, take the Hutchinson River Parkway north from the Bronx Whitestone Bridge and turn east on the Bronx Pelham Parkway, which turns into Shore Road. From Shore Road, follow the signs to City Island and drive the island's length on City Island Avenue.

The following are several sites that almost don't belong in the city—the "unconcrete" spots that make you feel as if you were somewhere else.

- The Cloisters: Fort Tyron Park, north of the George Washington Bridge and east of the Henry Hudson Parkway.
- Bronx Zoo and Botanical Garden: Bronx Park off Fordham Road or the Bronx River Parkway—often crowded but a nice zoo.
- Wave Hill: 675 W. 252nd Street, in the Bronx, a 28-acre estate that overlooks the Hudson River and offers tranquil walks through gardens surrounding the picturesque manor house.
- Hudson River tours: Any of the Hudson River tours in upstate New York provide get-a-way trips for city dwellers. Garrison, a quaint village off U.S. Route 9 (see *Cross-state drives, New York*), makes a perfect day trip and can be reached in about an hour and a half from midtown.

Newark

Newark is so often maligned that it seems only fair to put in a good word for the city here. Not expecting to put an end to all Newark jokes, I include the "Magical History Tour" laid out by Essex County. Leading drivers on a tour of urban areas surprisingly close to rural New Jersey, the route winds through some attractive suburbs and past almost unlimited historic sites. The circle is only about 50 miles, but to do justice to the points of interest along it you should allow a whole day. It really is a sightseeing tour, not a scenic through-route.

Starting in Newark, you pass some late nineteenth-century structures, leaving the city to enter South Orange, Maplewood, and Millburn. There's a "George Washington Slept Here" house and a historic paper mill now used as a playhouse. You'll drive through the town of Livingston and then into Chepeside. Several theories explain the origin of this neighborhood's name. One states that this low, swampy area was the cheap side of town, while another says that the town is named after its markets, from the Old English word *chepe*, which meant "market." A third says the name actually was Sheepside, for the sheep that were pastured there.

You'll have a chance to see fossilized dinosaur footprints at Riker Hill Quarry in Roseland, along with historic houses and churches in Caldwell, Fairfield, and Montclair. This is the land of the Watchung Mountains, with low wetlands lying in the former bed of a glacial lake at their feet. Saying Watchung Mountains is akin to saying "pizza pie"—*Watchung* comes from an Indian word meaning "mountain."

For a dramatic view of New York City, you can drive to Montclair's Eagle Rock Reservation, former mountain aerie of the majestic birds.

From here back to Newark, it's more of the same—historic sites tucked among city structures, and some surprisingly scenic views. For details and a map of this interesting trip, contact Essex County's tourism department.

Philadelphia

Not a fraction of the space necessary to list all the historic sites in Philadelphia is available here. There are literally whole books devoted to the subject. Much of the area surrounding the city is mountain land and worth a drive to see it in detail (see *Scenic drives, Southeastern Pennsylvania*).

Pittsburgh

For scenic drives you're better off staying far from the city boundaries, but if you want an enlightening look at the Ohio River, take Route 65 northwest to Pittsburgh through Allegheny and Beaver counties. From Pittsburgh to Beaver Falls, the drive is about 35 miles long.

Baltimore

Often called the "Monumental City" for its statues dedicated to the likes of Washington, Columbus, and Francis Scott Key, Baltimore is full of historic sites of all sizes, ages, and types. The place is also full of battlefields. Downtown Baltimore is not architecturally appealing, but it does offer some excellent area museums. The city tour listed below takes in just a few of the more interesting spots and gives a view of this awesome harbor.

Washington Monument, Baltimore.
(This and all photographs in this chapter courtesy of Maryland Office of Tourist Development)

The B & O Railroad Museum, Baltimore.

Historic sites and harbor views

This trip, only three or four miles long, can be extended to include other Baltimore sites you'd like to see. Start on Amity Street, off Lexington Street, to find the Edgar Allan Poe House. Poe lived there for only three years, 1832-35, but the house has been restored and now functions as a museum.

Drive east on Lexington Street to Greene Street and turn right. Turn left on Fayette Street. At the corner of Greene and Fayette, you can see Poe's grave. Originally a nondescript tomb at the rear of Westminster Churchyard, the grave was moved to the yard's entrance and a tomb erected with funds raised by local teachers and students.

Turn left on Paca Street. At the northeast corner of Lexington and Paca is the Lexington Market. It's been there since 1803, and some of the stalls are run by descendants of the original families that operated them. Nearly every kind of locally available food can be found here.

Turn right on Lexington Street and drive to Liberty Street. Turn right and drive to Baltimore Street. Turn left and pass Charles Center, an impressively modern multipurpose complex that includes office space and apartments, among other things. Turn right on Charles Street, drive past Lombard Street, and turn left on Pratt Street. Turn right on Light Street to the Inner Harbor. There you can see the U.S. Frigate *Constellation,* the first commissioned ship of the U.S. Navy. Dated 1797, the *Constellation* is the oldest American vessel continuously afloat.

In Baltimore's inner harbor you can see the frigate *Constellation,* first commissioned ship in the U.S. Navy.

Turn left on Key Highway and drive to Federal Hill, a popular overlook from which to view the city skyline. On nearby Montgomery Street many historic homes are being restored.

Round the curve and continue south on Key Highway to Fort McHenry. To get out to the fort, take Fort Avenue off the highway. During the Battle of Baltimore, September 12-13, 1814, Francis Scott Key saw the flag that inspired him to write the national anthem.

Washington, D.C.

Washington is really a lovely city, with its gleaming white monuments, wide Potomac River, and charming houses in neighborhoods like Georgetown. Yet, D.C. is still a city, and it's no mean feat to find a little-traveled route through the area. (For routes and points of interest surrounding the capital, see *Scenic drives, Central Maryland.*)

Rock Creek Parkway

Rock Creek Parkway is as close as D.C. roads come to scenic; this one really deserves the label. Running the length of Rock Creek Park, the road is printed on only a few maps, but it is popular with area drivers. The route is scenic only during nonpeak traffic hours. This narrows down the best driving time to the late night hours and not much more. You might try a winter or rainy afternoon, far from either rush hour, but don't be surprised if you do run into *some* traffic.

Rock Creek Park runs about 25 miles from Upper Montgomery County to the Lincoln Memorial in D.C., forming a 4,000-acre natural green swath that cuts through the city. It's a good transcity alternate to Connecticut Avenue or 16th Street (Route 29), both entering the city from Maryland. From Silver Spring you can take Kalmia Road west from Route 29 (Alaska Avenue and 16th Street) and turn left on the parkway after crossing the creek. From the Chevy Chase area, follow Route 410 east and turn right on the parkway before you come to the creek.

The parkway hugs the creek all the way into town, passing a

golf course to the east and the famous national Zoological Garden (about halfway into D.C.).

When you reach the Lincoln Memorial, you can check out the reflecting pool and the Washington Monument on the mall. From there you can continue your tour by driving south on Ohio Street from the Lincoln Memorial, past the Tidal Basin, the Jefferson Memorial, West Potomac Park, Lady Byrd Johnson Park, and East Potomac Park golf course—all in about two miles—to Hains Point on the water.

Index